CW01512178

ARIES
PATH
YOUR DAILY 2025 HOROSCOPE GUIDE

AMANDA M CLARKE

Daily Guidance
SERIES

Welcome to The Aries Path: Your Daily 2025 Horoscope Guide—a powerful and energetic companion designed specifically for those born under the bold and dynamic sign of Aries. Known for your courage, determination, and independent spirit, this book will guide you through 2025 with daily horoscopes that align with your fiery nature.

Each day's horoscope offers practical insights into love, career, health, and personal growth, empowering you to make the most of every opportunity. Whether you're seeking to conquer new goals or enhance your personal relationships, this guide provides the cosmic wisdom and motivational affirmations to help you thrive.

Embrace the journey ahead, Aries—2025 is yours to take on!

ARIES
March 21 - April 19

2025
Overview

Aries in 2025
Overview

Aries, 2025 is a year of action, growth, and bold new beginnings. Your natural drive and courage will be rewarded as opportunities for success emerge, particularly in your career and personal projects. Early in the year, you'll feel motivated to take on challenges and pursue your goals with fierce determination. Relationships, both personal and professional, will benefit from your openness and leadership.

Mid-year brings opportunities for travel or personal adventures, igniting your adventurous spirit. While you'll be busy achieving your ambitions, don't forget to prioritize balance and self-care to avoid burnout.

By the end of 2025, you'll feel empowered, having made significant progress in multiple areas of your life, and ready to take on the future with confidence.

Aries in 2025
Love and Relationships

Aries, 2025 promises excitement, growth, and emotional depth in your love life. For those in relationships, this year will be a time of strengthening your bond through open communication and shared experiences. You'll be more inclined to take the lead, bringing passion and energy into your connection. Just be mindful of your partner's needs, allowing space for them to express themselves too.

For single Aries, 2025 brings thrilling new romantic opportunities. Your boldness and confidence will attract potential partners, especially mid-year when the stars favor new connections. Don't be afraid to pursue what feels right—your intuition will guide you to fulfilling relationships.

Overall, this year fosters growth in both new and existing relationships, encouraging you to open your heart and connect on deeper levels.

Aries in 2025
Career

Aries, 2025 is a year of career breakthroughs and bold moves. Your natural leadership and determination will put you in the spotlight, opening doors for advancement, promotions, or new ventures. Early in the year, opportunities for growth will emerge, particularly in roles that challenge your skills and push you to step out of your comfort zone.

Mid-year brings chances to collaborate with others or take on a leadership position, allowing you to showcase your talents. Trust your instincts when making decisions, and don't shy away from taking calculated risks—they may lead to significant rewards.

By the end of 2025, you'll see tangible progress in your career, feeling more confident, successful, and aligned with your professional goals.

Aries in 2025
Wealth

Aries, 2025 brings promising financial growth and opportunities to build long-term stability. Early in the year, you'll feel motivated to take control of your finances, setting clear goals and exploring new investment opportunities. Your bold and proactive approach will help you make smart decisions that increase your income, whether through career advancement, side ventures, or smart investments.

Mid-year, unexpected financial opportunities may arise, allowing you to grow your savings or make significant purchases. However, it's essential to balance your ambitious nature with careful planning—avoid impulsive spending and focus on building a solid foundation.

By the end of 2025, your financial situation will feel more secure and rewarding, thanks to your focus on strategic growth and long-term wealth building.

Aries in 2025
Health

Aries, 2025 is a year to prioritize balance and overall well-being. With your energetic and fast-paced lifestyle, maintaining good health will be key to keeping up with your ambitions. Early in the year, focus on creating a consistent fitness routine and improving your diet to boost energy levels.

Mid-year may bring a surge in activity, so be mindful not to overexert yourself. Make time for rest and recovery to avoid burnout. Stress management will also be essential—practices like meditation, yoga, or simply taking breaks will help maintain your mental well-being.

By the end of 2025, with a balance of activity and self-care, you'll feel stronger, more centered, and ready to tackle new challenges with full vitality.

Aries in 2025
Study

Aries, 2025 is a year of intellectual growth and learning. Whether you're pursuing formal education or enhancing your skills for personal or professional development, your natural drive and enthusiasm will help you excel. Early in the year, you'll feel motivated to dive into new subjects or revisit old passions with renewed energy.

Mid-year, opportunities for learning through hands-on experience or practical application may arise, giving you the chance to deepen your knowledge. Stay focused and disciplined, as your natural inclination to take action will push you to achieve great results in your studies.

By the end of 2025, your hard work and dedication will lead to significant progress, setting you up for future success in both personal and professional areas.

This book is dedicated to you,

Charmaine

Much love and gratitude, for your unwavering friendship, fierce loyalty, and the adventurous path you walk.
Here's to all the incredible moments we've shared and the many more to come!
xxx

ARIES
DAILY HOROSCOPE

2025

January
2025

Aries

1 January 2025

Dear Aries, today's energy sparks new beginnings, making it the perfect time to set your intentions for the year ahead. With your natural drive and determination, you're poised to make big strides in your personal and professional life. Take a moment to reflect on your long-term goals and ensure your actions align with your aspirations. Today is all about harnessing your fiery energy and embracing opportunities.

Affirmation & Gratitude

I embrace new beginnings with enthusiasm, knowing that my determination will lead me to achieve my goals.

Aries

2 January 2025

Dear Aries, focus on relationships today. Whether it's with family, friends, or colleagues, meaningful conversations will deepen your emotional connections. Take the lead in communication and be open to listening. Today's energy encourages you to show empathy and build stronger bonds. Trust that your authentic self will inspire those around you.

Affirmation & Gratitude

I strengthen my relationships by being open, honest, and empathetic, creating deeper emotional connections with those who matter to me.

Aries

3 January 2025

Dear Aries, career progress is in the spotlight today, and your ambition shines through. Whether you're seeking new opportunities or advancing in your current role, take decisive steps toward your professional goals. Stay focused, and trust that your hard work will lead to success. Embrace your leadership qualities and don't be afraid to take charge.

Affirmation & Gratitude

I trust in my abilities and leadership, knowing that my hard work will lead to career growth and fulfillment.

Aries

4 January 2025

Dear Aries, financial planning takes priority today. Reassess your budget and ensure your spending aligns with your long-term goals. Today's energy supports responsible decisions that will bring stability and peace of mind. Avoid impulsive purchases and focus on securing your financial future.

Affirmation & Gratitude

I make thoughtful financial decisions that bring stability and security into my life, ensuring a peaceful future.

Aries

5 January 2025

Dear Aries, creativity flows freely today, making it a perfect time to explore new ideas and express your vision. Whether you're working on personal projects or solving challenges, let your imagination guide you. Trust your instincts and embrace bold, innovative thinking.

Affirmation & Gratitude

I trust in my creativity, knowing that bold ideas will lead to exciting breakthroughs and fulfilling outcomes.

Aries

6 January 2025

Dear Aries, relationships take center stage today. Focus on nurturing emotional connections with loved ones, whether you're reconnecting with family, friends, or a romantic partner. Meaningful conversations will strengthen your bonds. Be present, listen with empathy, and share your thoughts openly.

Affirmation & Gratitude

I nurture my relationships with love, honesty, and gratitude, creating deeper emotional connections with those who bring joy into my life.

Aries

7 January 2025

Dear Aries, career advancement is within reach today. Take bold steps toward your professional goals, whether you're seeking new responsibilities or exploring new opportunities. Stay confident in your abilities and trust that your hard work will lead to success.

Affirmation & Gratitude

I trust in my skills and dedication, knowing they will lead to career growth and personal fulfillment.

Aries

8 January 2025

Dear Aries, financial matters come into focus today, and the energy supports making responsible decisions that align with your long-term goals. Whether you're reassessing your budget or planning for a significant purchase, thoughtful financial choices today will bring peace and security.

Affirmation & Gratitude

I make responsible financial decisions that ensure peace, stability, and security in my future.

Aries

9 January 2025

Dear Aries, creativity is heightened today, making it a perfect time to explore new ideas and bring your vision to life. Whether you're working on personal projects or artistic endeavors, today's energy supports bold, imaginative thinking. Let your creativity guide you.

Affirmation & Gratitude

I trust in my creativity, knowing that bold ideas will lead to exciting breakthroughs and fulfilling outcomes.

Aries

10 January 2025

Dear Aries, relationships take focus today, and the energy supports deepening emotional connections with loved ones. Whether you're spending time with family or nurturing a romantic bond, meaningful conversations will strengthen your relationships. Be open and honest in your interactions.

Affirmation & Gratitude

I nurture my relationships with love, empathy, and gratitude, creating deeper emotional bonds with those who bring joy into my life.

Aries

11 January 2025

Dear Aries, career growth is highlighted today, and the energy encourages you to take decisive steps toward your professional goals. Whether you're seeking a promotion or taking on new responsibilities, today's energy favors proactive action. Stay confident in your abilities.

Affirmation & Gratitude

I trust in my skills and hard work, knowing they will lead to career success and fulfillment.

Aries

12 January 2025

Dear Aries, financial planning takes center stage today, and the cosmos encourages you to make thoughtful decisions about your future. Whether you're reassessing your savings plan or preparing for a large purchase, today's energy supports responsible choices. Avoid impulsive spending and focus on long-term security.

Affirmation & Gratitude

I make thoughtful financial decisions that ensure peace, stability, and security in my future.

Aries

13 January 2025

Dear Aries, creativity is flowing today, making it an ideal time to explore new ideas and express your vision. Whether you're working on personal projects, solving challenges, or pursuing artistic endeavors, today's energy supports bold, imaginative thinking. Let your creativity guide you toward exciting breakthroughs.

Affirmation & Gratitude

I trust in my creativity, knowing that bold ideas will lead to exciting opportunities and fulfilling outcomes.

Aries

14 January 2025

Dear Aries, relationships take focus today, and the energy supports nurturing deeper emotional connections with loved ones. Whether you're reconnecting with family, spending time with friends, or deepening a romantic bond, meaningful conversations will strengthen your relationships. Be present, listen with empathy, and express your thoughts openly.

Affirmation & Gratitude

I nurture my relationships with love, empathy, and gratitude, creating deeper emotional bonds with those who bring joy into my life.

Aries

15 January 2025

Dear Aries, career growth is in the spotlight today, and the cosmos supports making bold moves toward your professional goals. Whether you're expanding your skills, seeking a promotion, or exploring new responsibilities, today's energy favors proactive action. Trust in your abilities and take steps toward success.

Affirmation & Gratitude

I trust in my hard work and skills, knowing they will lead to career success and personal fulfillment.

Aries

16 January 2025

Dear Aries, financial matters take priority today, and the energy supports making responsible decisions that align with your long-term goals. Whether you're reassessing your budget or preparing for future investments, thoughtful choices today will bring peace and stability.

Affirmation & Gratitude

I make responsible financial decisions that ensure peace, stability, and security in my future.

Aries

17 January 2025

Dear Aries, creativity is heightened today, making it a great time to explore new ideas and bring your vision to life. Whether you're working on personal projects, solving challenges, or pursuing artistic endeavors, today's energy supports bold, imaginative thinking. Let your creativity flow freely.

Affirmation & Gratitude

I trust in my creative energy, knowing that bold ideas will lead to exciting opportunities and fulfilling outcomes.

Aries

18 January 2025

Dear Aries, relationships take center stage today, and the cosmos supports building stronger emotional connections with loved ones. Whether you're spending time with family, nurturing friendships, or focusing on a romantic relationship, meaningful conversations will bring you closer to those who matter most.

Affirmation & Gratitude

I nurture my relationships with love, empathy, and honesty, creating deeper emotional bonds with those who bring joy into my life.

Aries

19 January 2025

Dear Aries, career advancement is highlighted today, and the energy supports making bold moves toward your professional aspirations. Whether you're seeking a promotion, expanding your responsibilities, or exploring new opportunities, today's energy favors success. Stay confident and proactive.

Affirmation & Gratitude

I trust in my hard work and dedication, knowing they will lead to career success and fulfillment.

Aries

20 January 2025

Dear Aries, financial planning is in focus today, and the energy supports making responsible decisions that align with your long-term financial goals. Whether you're saving for future investments or reassessing your budget, today's energy favors thoughtful financial planning. Focus on long-term stability.

Affirmation & Gratitude

I make responsible financial decisions that bring peace, stability, and security to my future.

Aries

21 January 2025

Dear Aries, creativity flows effortlessly today, making it the perfect time to explore new ideas and express your vision. Whether you're working on personal projects, solving challenges, or pursuing artistic endeavors, today's energy supports bold, imaginative thinking. Let your creativity guide you toward success.

Affirmation & Gratitude

I trust in my creativity, knowing that bold ideas will lead to exciting breakthroughs and fulfilling outcomes.

Aries

22 January 2025

Dear Aries, relationships take priority today, and the cosmos supports building deeper emotional connections with loved ones. Whether you're reconnecting with family, spending time with friends, or focusing on a romantic bond, meaningful conversations will strengthen your relationships. Be open, honest, and empathetic in your interactions.

Affirmation & Gratitude

I nurture my relationships with love, honesty, and gratitude, creating deeper emotional connections with those who bring joy into my life.

Aries

23 January 2025

Dear Aries, career growth is highlighted today, and the energy supports making bold moves toward your professional goals. Whether you're expanding your skill set, seeking new responsibilities, or exploring new opportunities, today's energy favors proactive action. Be confident in your abilities and stay focused on your aspirations.

Affirmation & Gratitude

I trust in my skills and dedication, knowing they will lead to career success and long-term growth.

Aries

24 January 2025

Dear Aries, financial planning takes priority today, and the energy supports making responsible decisions that align with your long-term financial goals. Whether you're saving for future investments, reassessing your budget, or preparing for major purchases, today's energy favors thoughtful financial choices. Focus on long-term stability.

Affirmation & Gratitude

I make thoughtful financial decisions that ensure peace, stability, and security in my future.

Aries

25 January 2025

Dear Aries, creativity flows effortlessly today, making it the perfect time to explore new ideas and express your vision. Whether you're working on personal projects, solving challenges, or pursuing artistic endeavors, today's energy supports bold, imaginative thinking. Let your creativity guide you toward success.

Affirmation & Gratitude

I trust in my creativity, knowing that bold ideas will lead to exciting breakthroughs and fulfilling outcomes.

Aries

26 January 2025

Dear Aries, relationships are the focus today, and the energy supports building deeper emotional connections with loved ones. Whether you're reconnecting with family, nurturing friendships, or focusing on a romantic bond, meaningful conversations will strengthen your relationships. Be present, listen with empathy, and share your feelings openly.

Affirmation & Gratitude

I nurture my relationships with love, empathy, and honesty, creating deeper emotional bonds with those who bring joy into my life.

Aries

27 January 2025

Dear Aries, career growth is highlighted today, and the energy supports making bold moves toward your professional goals. Whether you're seeking a promotion, expanding your responsibilities, or exploring new opportunities, today's energy favors proactive action. Trust in your abilities and stay focused on your aspirations.

Affirmation & Gratitude

I trust in my skills and dedication, knowing they will lead to career success and long-term growth.

Aries

28 January 2025

Dear Aries, financial matters come into focus today, and the energy supports making thoughtful decisions that align with your long-term financial goals. Whether you're preparing for a major purchase or reassessing your budget, today's energy favors responsible financial choices. Focus on long-term security.

Affirmation & Gratitude

I make responsible financial decisions that bring peace, stability, and security into my future.

Aries

29 January 2025

Dear Aries, creativity is heightened today, making it the perfect time to explore new ideas and express your unique vision. Whether you're working on personal projects, solving challenges, or pursuing artistic endeavors, today's energy supports bold, imaginative thinking. Let your creativity flow freely.

Affirmation & Gratitude

I trust in my creative energy, knowing that bold ideas will lead to exciting breakthroughs and fulfilling outcomes.

Aries

30 January 2025

Dear Aries, relationships take focus today, and the cosmos encourages you to nurture emotional connections with loved ones. Whether you're reconnecting with family or spending time with friends, meaningful conversations will bring harmony and joy. Be present and listen with empathy.

Affirmation & Gratitude

I nurture my relationships with love, honesty, and gratitude, creating deeper emotional connections with those who bring joy into my life.

Aries

31 January 2025

Dear Aries, career progress is in the spotlight today, and the energy supports making bold moves toward your professional goals. Whether you're seeking a promotion, expanding your responsibilities, or exploring new opportunities, today's energy favors proactive action. Stay confident in your abilities and trust your dedication.

Affirmation & Gratitude

I trust in my hard work and skills, knowing they will lead to career success and personal fulfillment.

February

2025

Aries

I February 2025

Dear Aries, creativity takes center stage today, making it a perfect time to explore new ideas and bring your vision to life. Whether you're working on personal projects, artistic endeavors, or solving challenges, today's energy supports bold, imaginative thinking. Trust in your ability to bring new concepts to reality.

Affirmation & Gratitude

I trust in my creativity, knowing that bold ideas will lead to exciting breakthroughs and fulfilling outcomes.

Aries

2 February 2025

Dear Aries, relationships take focus today, and the energy supports deepening emotional connections with loved ones. Whether you're reconnecting with family or nurturing friendships, meaningful conversations will bring you closer to those who matter most. Be open and empathetic.

Affirmation & Gratitude

I nurture my relationships with love, honesty, and gratitude, creating deeper emotional bonds with those who bring joy into my life.

Aries

3 February 2025

Dear Aries, career growth is highlighted today, and the cosmos encourages you to take bold steps toward your professional goals. Whether you're seeking new responsibilities, exploring opportunities, or expanding your skills, today's energy favors proactive action. Stay confident in your abilities.

Affirmation & Gratitude

I trust in my skills and hard work, knowing they will lead to career success and personal fulfillment.

Aries

4 February 2025

Dear Aries, financial planning takes priority today, and the energy supports making responsible decisions that align with your long-term financial goals. Whether you're reassessing your budget or preparing for a major purchase, thoughtful financial choices today will bring peace and security.

Affirmation & Gratitude

I make responsible financial decisions that bring stability and security into my life.

Aries

5 February 2025

Dear Aries, creativity is heightened today, making it the perfect time to explore new ideas and express your vision. Whether you're working on personal projects, solving challenges, or pursuing artistic endeavors, today's energy supports bold, imaginative thinking. Let your creativity guide you.

Affirmation & Gratitude

I trust in my creative energy, knowing that bold ideas will lead to exciting opportunities and fulfilling outcomes.

Aries

6 February 2025

Dear Aries, relationships take priority today, and the cosmos supports building deeper emotional connections with loved ones. Whether you're reconnecting with family, spending time with friends, or deepening a romantic bond, meaningful conversations will strengthen your relationships. Be present, listen with empathy, and express your thoughts openly.

Affirmation & Gratitude

I nurture my relationships with love, empathy, and honesty, creating deeper emotional connections with those who bring joy into my life.

Aries

7 February 2025

Dear Aries, career advancement is within reach today, and the energy supports making bold moves toward your professional goals. Whether you're expanding your skills or seeking new responsibilities, today's energy favors success. Stay proactive and confident in your abilities.

Affirmation & Gratitude

I trust in my skills and dedication, knowing they will lead to career success and fulfillment.

Aries

8 February 2025

Dear Aries, financial matters come into focus today, and the energy supports making responsible decisions that align with your long-term financial goals. Whether you're saving for future investments or reassessing your budget, thoughtful choices today will bring peace and security.

Affirmation & Gratitude

I make responsible financial decisions that ensure peace, stability, and security in my future.

Aries

9 February 2025

Dear Aries, creativity flows effortlessly today, making it an ideal time to explore new ideas and bring your vision to life. Whether you're working on personal projects, solving challenges, or pursuing artistic endeavors, today's energy supports bold, imaginative thinking. Let your creativity guide you toward success.

Affirmation & Gratitude

I trust in my creativity, knowing that bold ideas will lead to exciting breakthroughs and fulfilling outcomes.

Aries

10 February 2025

Dear Aries, relationships take focus today, and the energy supports nurturing deeper emotional connections with loved ones. Whether you're reconnecting with family, spending time with friends, or focusing on a romantic bond, meaningful conversations will strengthen your relationships. Be open and empathetic.

Affirmation & Gratitude

I nurture my relationships with love, honesty, and gratitude, creating deeper emotional connections with those who bring joy into my life.

Aries

11 February 2025

Dear Aries, career growth is highlighted today, and the energy supports making bold moves toward your professional goals. Whether you're expanding your skills, seeking new responsibilities, or exploring new opportunities, today's energy favors proactive action. Trust in your abilities and stay focused on your aspirations.

Affirmation & Gratitude

I trust in my skills and dedication, knowing they will lead to career success and long-term growth.

Aries

12 February 2025

Dear Aries, financial planning takes priority today, and the energy supports making responsible decisions that align with your long-term financial goals. Whether you're saving for future investments or reassessing your budget, today's energy favors thoughtful financial planning. Focus on long-term security.

Affirmation & Gratitude

I make thoughtful financial decisions that ensure peace, stability, and security in my future.

Aries

13 February 2025

Dear Aries, creativity is heightened today, making it a perfect time to explore new ideas and express your unique vision. Whether you're working on personal projects, solving challenges, or pursuing artistic endeavors, today's energy supports bold, imaginative thinking. Let your creativity flow freely.

Affirmation & Gratitude

I trust in my creative energy, knowing that bold ideas will lead to exciting breakthroughs and fulfilling outcomes.

Aries

14 February 2025

Dear Aries, relationships take priority today, and the energy supports building deeper emotional connections with loved ones. Whether you're reconnecting with family, spending time with friends, or focusing on a romantic bond, meaningful conversations will bring harmony and joy. Be present, listen with empathy, and share your feelings.

Affirmation & Gratitude

I nurture my relationships with love, honesty, and empathy, creating deeper emotional bonds with those who bring joy into my life.

Aries

15 February 2025

Dear Aries, career progress is highlighted today, and the energy supports making bold moves toward your professional goals. Whether you're expanding your responsibilities or seeking a promotion, today's energy favors proactive action. Stay confident in your abilities and trust your dedication.

Affirmation & Gratitude

I trust in my hard work and skills, knowing they will lead to career success and personal fulfillment.

Aries

16 February 2025

Dear Aries, financial matters take center stage today, and the energy supports making responsible decisions that align with your long-term goals. Whether you're reassessing your budget or saving for future investments, thoughtful planning today will bring peace and stability.

Affirmation & Gratitude

I make thoughtful financial decisions that ensure peace, stability, and security in my future.

Aries

17 February 2025

Dear Aries, creativity flows effortlessly today, making it a great time to explore new ideas and express your vision. Whether you're working on personal projects, solving challenges, or pursuing artistic endeavors, today's energy supports bold, imaginative thinking. Let your creativity guide you.

Affirmation & Gratitude

I trust in my creativity, knowing that bold ideas will lead to exciting breakthroughs and fulfilling outcomes.

Aries

18 February 2025

Dear Aries, relationships take focus today, and the energy supports nurturing deeper emotional connections with loved ones. Whether you're reconnecting with family, spending time with friends, or focusing on a romantic relationship, meaningful conversations will strengthen your bonds. Be open and empathetic.

Affirmation & Gratitude

I nurture my relationships with love, empathy, and gratitude, creating deeper emotional connections with those who bring joy into my life.

Aries

19 February 2025

Dear Aries, career growth is in the spotlight today, and the energy supports making bold moves toward your professional goals. Whether you're seeking a promotion, expanding your skills, or exploring new opportunities, today's energy favors proactive action. Trust in your abilities and stay focused on success.

Affirmation & Gratitude

I trust in my hard work and skills, knowing they will lead to career success and personal fulfillment.

Aries

20 February 2025

Dear Aries, financial planning takes priority today, and the cosmos encourages you to make responsible decisions about your future. Whether you're reassessing your savings, planning for a major purchase, or preparing for investments, today's energy supports responsible financial choices.

Affirmation & Gratitude

I make responsible financial decisions that ensure peace, stability, and security for my future.

Aries

21 February 2025

Dear Aries, creativity is heightened today, making it the perfect time to explore new ideas and express your vision. Whether you're working on personal projects, solving challenges, or pursuing artistic endeavors, today's energy supports bold, imaginative thinking. Let your creativity flow freely.

Affirmation & Gratitude

I trust in my creativity, knowing that bold ideas will lead to exciting breakthroughs and fulfilling outcomes.

Aries

22 February 2025

Dear Aries, relationships take focus today, and the energy supports deepening emotional connections with loved ones. Whether you're spending time with family, nurturing friendships, or focusing on a romantic bond, meaningful conversations will strengthen your relationships. Be present, listen with empathy, and share your thoughts openly.

Affirmation & Gratitude

I nurture my relationships with love, honesty, and gratitude, creating deeper emotional bonds with those who bring joy into my life.

Aries

23 February 2025

Dear Aries, career advancement is within reach today, and the energy supports making bold moves toward your professional goals. Whether you're expanding your responsibilities, seeking new opportunities, or exploring new skills, today's energy favors success. Stay proactive and trust in your abilities.

Affirmation & Gratitude

I trust in my skills and dedication, knowing they will lead to career success and long-term fulfillment.

Aries

24 February 2025

Dear Aries, financial matters come into focus today, and the energy supports making responsible decisions that align with your long-term financial goals. Whether you're reassessing your budget, saving for future investments, or preparing for a significant purchase, today's energy favors responsible financial planning.

Affirmation & Gratitude

I make responsible financial decisions that bring peace, stability, and security to my future.

Aries

25 February 2025

Dear Aries, creativity is flowing effortlessly today, making it an ideal time to explore new ideas and bring your vision to life. Whether you're working on personal projects, solving challenges, or pursuing artistic endeavors, today's energy supports bold, imaginative thinking. Let your creativity guide you.

Affirmation & Gratitude

I trust in my creativity, knowing that bold ideas will lead to exciting breakthroughs and fulfilling outcomes.

Aries

26 February 2025

Dear Aries, relationships take priority today, and the energy supports building stronger emotional connections with loved ones. Whether you're reconnecting with family, spending time with friends, or focusing on a romantic bond, meaningful conversations will strengthen your relationships. Be open, honest, and empathetic.

Affirmation & Gratitude

I nurture my relationships with love, empathy, and gratitude, creating deeper emotional connections with those who bring joy into my life.

Aries

27 February 2025

Dear Aries, career progress is highlighted today, and the cosmos encourages you to take bold steps toward your professional goals. Whether you're seeking a promotion, expanding your responsibilities, or exploring new opportunities, today's energy favors proactive action. Trust in your abilities and take steps toward success.

Affirmation & Gratitude

I trust in my skills and dedication, knowing they will lead to career growth and personal fulfillment.

Aries

28 February 2025

Dear Aries, financial planning is in focus today, and the energy supports making responsible decisions that align with your long-term financial goals. Whether you're saving for future investments or reassessing your budget, today's energy favors thoughtful financial choices. Focus on building long-term stability.

Affirmation & Gratitude

I make responsible financial decisions that ensure peace, stability, and security in my future.

March

2025

Aries

1 March 2025

Dear Aries, creativity takes center stage today, making it the perfect time to explore new ideas and express your vision. Whether you're working on personal projects, artistic endeavors, or solving challenges, today's energy supports bold, imaginative thinking. Trust in your unique perspective to guide you toward exciting breakthroughs.

Affirmation & Gratitude

I trust in my creativity, knowing that bold ideas will lead to exciting opportunities and fulfilling outcomes.

Aries

2 March 2025

Dear Aries, relationships take focus today, and the energy supports nurturing deeper emotional connections with loved ones. Whether you're reconnecting with family, nurturing friendships, or focusing on a romantic bond, meaningful conversations will strengthen your relationships. Be present, listen with empathy, and share your thoughts openly.

Affirmation & Gratitude

I nurture my relationships with love, honesty, and gratitude, creating deeper emotional connections with those who bring joy into my life.

Aries

3 March 2025

Dear Aries, career progress is in the spotlight today, and the energy supports making bold moves toward your professional goals. Whether you're seeking new responsibilities, expanding your skill set, or exploring new opportunities, today's energy favors proactive action. Stay confident in your abilities and take steps toward success.

Affirmation & Gratitude

I trust in my hard work and dedication, knowing they will lead to career success and personal fulfillment.

Aries

4 March 2025

Dear Aries, financial planning takes priority today, and the cosmos encourages you to make thoughtful decisions about your future. Whether you're reassessing your savings or preparing for a major purchase, today's energy supports responsible choices that align with your long-term goals.

Affirmation & Gratitude

I make responsible financial decisions that ensure peace, stability, and security for my future.

Aries

5 March 2025

Dear Aries, creativity flows effortlessly today, making it a perfect time to explore new ideas and express your vision. Whether you're working on personal projects, solving challenges, or pursuing artistic endeavors, today's energy supports bold, imaginative thinking. Trust your creative instincts.

Affirmation & Gratitude

I trust in my creativity, knowing that bold ideas will lead to exciting breakthroughs and fulfilling outcomes.

Aries

6 March 2025

Dear Aries, relationships take priority today, and the energy supports building stronger emotional connections with loved ones. Whether you're reconnecting with family, spending time with friends, or focusing on a romantic bond, meaningful conversations will strengthen your relationships. Be open, honest, and empathetic in your interactions.

Affirmation & Gratitude

I nurture my relationships with love, empathy, and gratitude, creating deeper emotional bonds with those who bring joy into my life.

Aries

7 March 2025

Dear Aries, career advancement is highlighted today, and the cosmos encourages you to take bold steps toward your professional goals. Whether you're seeking a promotion, expanding your skills, or exploring new responsibilities, today's energy favors success. Stay proactive and trust in your abilities.

Affirmation & Gratitude

I trust in my skills and dedication, knowing they will lead to career success and long-term fulfillment.

Aries

8 March 2025

Dear Aries, financial matters come into focus today, and the energy supports making responsible decisions that align with your long-term financial goals. Whether you're saving for future investments or reassessing your budget, thoughtful financial planning today will bring peace and security.

Affirmation & Gratitude

I make responsible financial decisions that ensure peace, stability, and security in my future.

Aries

9 March 2025

Dear Aries, creativity is heightened today, making it an ideal time to explore new ideas and bring your vision to life. Whether you're working on personal projects, solving challenges, or pursuing artistic endeavors, today's energy supports bold, imaginative thinking. Let your creativity flow freely.

Affirmation & Gratitude

I trust in my creativity, knowing that bold ideas will lead to exciting breakthroughs and fulfilling outcomes.

Aries

10 March 2025

Dear Aries, relationships take focus today, and the energy supports nurturing deeper emotional connections with loved ones. Whether you're spending time with family, nurturing friendships, or focusing on a romantic bond, meaningful conversations will strengthen your relationships. Be open and empathetic.

Affirmation & Gratitude

I nurture my relationships with love, honesty, and gratitude, creating deeper emotional bonds with those who bring joy into my life.

Aries

11 March 2025

Dear Aries, career growth is in the spotlight today, and the energy supports making bold moves toward your professional goals. Whether you're expanding your skill set, seeking new responsibilities, or exploring new opportunities, today's energy favors proactive action. Trust in your abilities and stay focused on your aspirations.

Affirmation & Gratitude

I trust in my skills and dedication, knowing they will lead to career success and long-term growth.

Aries

12 March 2025

Dear Aries, financial planning takes priority today, and the energy supports making responsible decisions that align with your long-term goals. Whether you're reassessing your budget or preparing for future investments, thoughtful financial choices today will bring peace and security.

Affirmation & Gratitude

I make responsible financial decisions that ensure peace, stability, and security in my future.

Aries

13 March 2025

Dear Aries, creativity flows effortlessly today, making it the perfect time to explore new ideas and express your vision. Whether you're working on personal projects, solving challenges, or pursuing artistic endeavors, today's energy supports bold, imaginative thinking. Let your creativity guide you.

Affirmation & Gratitude

I trust in my creativity, knowing that bold ideas will lead to exciting breakthroughs and fulfilling outcomes.

Aries

14 March 2025

Dear Aries, relationships take focus today, and the cosmos encourages you to nurture emotional connections with loved ones. Whether you're reconnecting with family or spending time with friends, meaningful conversations will bring harmony and joy. Be present and listen with empathy.

Affirmation & Gratitude

I nurture my relationships with love, honesty, and gratitude, creating deeper emotional connections with those who bring joy into my life.

Aries

15 March 2025

Dear Aries, career progress is in the spotlight today, and the energy supports making bold moves toward your professional goals. Whether you're seeking a promotion, expanding your responsibilities, or exploring new opportunities, today's energy favors proactive action. Stay confident in your abilities and trust your dedication.

Affirmation & Gratitude

I trust in my hard work and skills, knowing they will lead to career success and personal fulfillment.

Aries

16 March 2025

Dear Aries, financial matters take center stage today, and the cosmos encourages you to make responsible decisions about your future. Whether you're reassessing your savings, preparing for a major purchase, or planning for investments, today's energy favors thoughtful financial planning.

Affirmation & Gratitude

I make responsible financial decisions that ensure peace, stability, and security for my future.

Aries

17 March 2025

Dear Aries, creativity is heightened today, making it a great time to explore new ideas and express your vision. Whether you're working on personal projects, solving challenges, or pursuing artistic endeavors, today's energy supports bold, imaginative thinking. Let your creativity flow freely.

Affirmation & Gratitude

I trust in my creativity, knowing that bold ideas will lead to exciting breakthroughs and fulfilling outcomes.

Aries

18 March 2025

Dear Aries, relationships take priority today, and the energy supports building deeper emotional connections with loved ones. Whether you're reconnecting with family, nurturing friendships, or focusing on a romantic bond, meaningful conversations will strengthen your relationships. Be open, honest, and empathetic.

Affirmation & Gratitude

I nurture my relationships with love, empathy, and gratitude, creating deeper emotional bonds with those who bring joy into my life.

Aries

19 March 2025

Dear Aries, career advancement is highlighted today, and the cosmos encourages you to take bold steps toward your professional goals. Whether you're seeking a promotion, expanding your skills, or exploring new responsibilities, today's energy favors success. Stay proactive and trust in your abilities.

Affirmation & Gratitude

I trust in my skills and dedication, knowing they will lead to career success and long-term fulfillment.

Aries

20 March 2025

Dear Aries, financial matters come into focus today, and the energy supports making responsible decisions that align with your long-term financial goals. Whether you're saving for future investments, reassessing your budget, or preparing for a major purchase, thoughtful financial choices today will bring peace and stability.

Affirmation & Gratitude

I make responsible financial decisions that ensure peace, stability, and security in my future.

Aries

21 March 2025

Dear Aries, creativity is heightened today, making it a great time to explore new ideas and bring your vision to life. Whether you're working on personal projects, solving challenges, or pursuing artistic endeavors, today's energy supports bold, imaginative thinking. Let your creativity guide you.

Affirmation & Gratitude

I trust in my creativity, knowing that bold ideas will lead to exciting breakthroughs and fulfilling outcomes.

Aries

22 March 2025

Dear Aries, relationships take focus today, and the cosmos supports nurturing emotional connections with loved ones. Whether you're spending time with family or nurturing friendships, meaningful conversations will bring harmony and joy. Be present and listen with empathy.

Affirmation & Gratitude

I nurture my relationships with love, honesty, and gratitude, creating deeper emotional connections with those who bring joy into my life.

Aries

23 March 2025

Dear Aries, career progress is in the spotlight today, and the energy supports making bold moves toward your professional goals. Whether you're seeking new responsibilities or exploring new opportunities, today's energy favors proactive action. Stay confident in your abilities.

Affirmation & Gratitude

I trust in my hard work and skills, knowing they will lead to career success and personal fulfillment.

Aries

24 March 2025

Dear Aries, financial planning is in focus today, and the energy supports making responsible decisions that align with your long-term goals. Whether you're reassessing your budget or preparing for future investments, thoughtful financial planning will bring peace and stability.

Affirmation & Gratitude

I make responsible financial decisions that ensure peace, stability, and security in my future.

Aries

25 March 2025

Dear Aries, creativity flows effortlessly today, making it a great time to explore new ideas and express your vision. Whether you're working on personal projects, solving challenges, or pursuing artistic endeavors, today's energy supports bold, imaginative thinking. Let your creativity guide you.

Affirmation & Gratitude

I trust in my creativity, knowing that bold ideas will lead to exciting breakthroughs and fulfilling outcomes.

Aries

26 March 2025

Dear Aries, relationships take center stage today, and the energy supports deepening emotional connections with loved ones. Whether you're reconnecting with family, nurturing friendships, or focusing on a romantic bond, meaningful conversations will strengthen your relationships. Be open and empathetic.

Affirmation & Gratitude

I nurture my relationships with love, honesty, and empathy, creating deeper emotional bonds with those who bring joy into my life.

Aries

27 March 2025

Dear Aries, career advancement is highlighted today, and the cosmos encourages you to take bold steps toward your professional goals. Whether you're seeking a promotion or expanding your responsibilities, today's energy favors proactive action. Stay focused on success.

Affirmation & Gratitude

I trust in my skills and dedication, knowing they will lead to career success and long-term fulfillment.

Aries

28 March 2025

Dear Aries, financial matters come into focus today, and the energy supports making responsible decisions that align with your long-term financial goals. Whether you're saving for future investments, reassessing your budget, or preparing for a significant purchase, thoughtful financial choices will bring peace and security.

Affirmation & Gratitude

I make responsible financial decisions that ensure peace, stability, and security in my future.

Aries

29 March 2025

Dear Aries, creativity is heightened today, making it a great time to explore new ideas and express your vision. Whether you're working on personal projects, artistic endeavors, or solving challenges, today's energy supports bold, imaginative thinking. Let your creativity flow freely.

Affirmation & Gratitude

I trust in my creativity, knowing that bold ideas will lead to exciting breakthroughs and fulfilling outcomes.

Aries
30 March 2025

Dear Aries, relationships take priority today, and the cosmos encourages you to nurture emotional connections with loved ones. Whether you're reconnecting with family or focusing on friends, meaningful conversations will strengthen your bonds. Be open, honest, and empathetic.

Affirmation & Gratitude

I nurture my relationships with love, honesty, and gratitude, creating deeper emotional bonds with those who bring joy into my life.

Aries

31 March 2025

Dear Aries, career growth is highlighted today, and the energy supports making bold moves toward your professional aspirations. Whether you're seeking new responsibilities, expanding your skills, or exploring new opportunities, today's energy favors proactive action. Stay confident in your abilities.

Affirmation & Gratitude

I trust in my hard work and dedication, knowing they will lead to career success and fulfillment.

April

2025

Aries

1 April 2025

Dear Aries, creativity takes the spotlight today, making it a great time to explore new ideas and bring your visions to life. Whether you're working on personal projects or solving challenges, today's energy supports bold, imaginative thinking. Let your creativity guide you toward exciting breakthroughs.

Affirmation & Gratitude

I trust in my creativity, knowing that bold ideas will lead to exciting opportunities and fulfilling outcomes.

Aries

2 April 2025

Dear Aries, relationships take focus today, and the energy supports deepening emotional connections with loved ones. Whether you're reconnecting with family, friends, or focusing on a romantic bond, meaningful conversations will strengthen your relationships. Be open and empathetic.

Affirmation & Gratitude

I nurture my relationships with love, honesty, and gratitude, creating deeper emotional bonds with those who bring joy into my life.

Aries

3 April 2025

Dear Aries, career progress is in the spotlight today, and the cosmos supports making bold moves toward your professional goals. Whether you're seeking new opportunities or expanding your current responsibilities, today's energy favors proactive action. Stay confident in your abilities.

Affirmation & Gratitude

I trust in my skills and hard work, knowing they will lead to career success and personal fulfillment.

Aries
4 April 2025

Dear Aries, financial planning takes priority today, and the energy encourages you to make thoughtful decisions about your future. Whether you're reassessing your savings or preparing for significant investments, responsible choices today will bring peace and long-term stability.

Affirmation & Gratitude

I make responsible financial decisions that ensure peace, stability, and security in my future.

Aries

5 April 2025

Dear Aries, creativity flows effortlessly today, making it a perfect time to explore new ideas and express your vision. Whether you're working on personal projects, solving challenges, or pursuing artistic endeavors, today's energy supports bold, imaginative thinking. Let your creativity lead the way.

Affirmation & Gratitude

I trust in my creativity, knowing that bold ideas will lead to exciting breakthroughs and fulfilling outcomes.

Aries

6 April 2025

Dear Aries, relationships take priority today, and the cosmos supports building stronger emotional connections with loved ones. Whether you're reconnecting with family or nurturing friendships, meaningful conversations will strengthen your bonds. Be open, honest, and empathetic in your interactions.

Affirmation & Gratitude

I nurture my relationships with love, empathy, and honesty, creating deeper emotional connections with those who bring joy into my life.

Aries

7 April 2025

Dear Aries, career advancement is within reach today, and the energy supports making bold moves toward your professional goals. Whether you're expanding your responsibilities or seeking new opportunities, today's energy favors success. Stay proactive and trust your abilities.

Affirmation & Gratitude

I trust in my skills and dedication, knowing they will lead to career success and long-term fulfillment.

Aries

8 April 2025

Dear Aries, financial matters come into focus today, and the energy supports making responsible decisions that align with your long-term financial goals. Whether you're saving for future investments or reassessing your budget, thoughtful financial planning today will bring peace and security.

Affirmation & Gratitude

I make responsible financial decisions that ensure peace, stability, and security in my future.

Aries

9 April 2025

Dear Aries, creativity is heightened today, making it a perfect time to explore new ideas and bring your visions to life. Whether you're working on personal projects, solving challenges, or pursuing artistic endeavors, today's energy supports bold, imaginative thinking. Trust your instincts and let your creativity flow.

Affirmation & Gratitude

I trust in my creativity, knowing that bold ideas will lead to exciting breakthroughs and fulfilling outcomes.

Aries

10 April 2025

Dear Aries, relationships take focus today, and the energy supports deepening emotional connections with loved ones. Whether you're reconnecting with family or spending time with friends, meaningful conversations will strengthen your relationships. Be open and empathetic in your interactions.

Affirmation & Gratitude

I nurture my relationships with love, honesty, and gratitude, creating deeper emotional bonds with those who bring joy into my life.

Aries

11 April 2025

Dear Aries, career growth is in the spotlight today, and the cosmos encourages you to make bold moves toward your professional aspirations. Whether you're expanding your skills, seeking new responsibilities, or exploring new opportunities, today's energy favors proactive action. Trust in your abilities and stay focused on success.

Affirmation & Gratitude

I trust in my skills and hard work, knowing they will lead to career success and personal fulfillment.

Aries

12 April 2025

Dear Aries, financial planning takes priority today, and the cosmos supports making responsible decisions that align with your long-term financial goals. Whether you're reassessing your budget or saving for future investments, thoughtful choices today will bring peace and stability.

Affirmation & Gratitude

I make thoughtful financial decisions that ensure peace, stability, and security in my future.

Aries

13 April 2025

Dear Aries, creativity flows effortlessly today, making it the perfect time to explore new ideas and express your vision. Whether you're working on personal projects, solving challenges, or pursuing artistic endeavors, today's energy supports bold, imaginative thinking. Let your creativity guide you.

Affirmation & Gratitude

I trust in my creativity, knowing that bold ideas will lead to exciting breakthroughs and fulfilling outcomes.

Aries

14 April 2025

Dear Aries, relationships take focus today, and the energy supports nurturing deeper emotional connections with loved ones. Whether you're reconnecting with family, spending time with friends, or focusing on a romantic bond, meaningful conversations will strengthen your relationships. Be open, honest, and empathetic in your interactions.

Affirmation & Gratitude

I nurture my relationships with love, empathy, and gratitude, creating deeper emotional bonds with those who bring joy into my life.

Aries

15 April 2025

Dear Aries, career progress is in the spotlight today, and the cosmos encourages you to take bold steps toward your professional goals. Whether you're seeking a promotion, expanding your responsibilities, or exploring new opportunities, today's energy favors proactive action. Stay confident in your abilities and trust your dedication.

Affirmation & Gratitude

I trust in my hard work and skills, knowing they will lead to career success and fulfillment.

Aries

16 April 2025

Dear Aries, financial matters take center stage today, and the energy supports making responsible decisions about your future. Whether you're reassessing your savings, preparing for a major purchase, or planning for investments, today's energy favors thoughtful financial planning. Focus on long-term security.

Affirmation & Gratitude

I make responsible financial decisions that ensure peace, stability, and security in my future.

Aries

17 April 2025

Dear Aries, creativity is heightened today, making it a great time to explore new ideas and bring your vision to life. Whether you're working on personal projects, solving challenges, or pursuing artistic endeavors, today's energy supports bold, imaginative thinking. Let your creativity flow freely.

Affirmation & Gratitude

I trust in my creativity, knowing that bold ideas will lead to exciting breakthroughs and fulfilling outcomes.

Aries

18 April 2025

Dear Aries, relationships take focus today, and the energy supports deepening emotional connections with loved ones. Whether you're spending time with family, nurturing friendships, or focusing on a romantic bond, meaningful conversations will strengthen your relationships. Be present and listen with empathy.

Affirmation & Gratitude

I nurture my relationships with love, honesty, and gratitude, creating deeper emotional connections with those who bring joy into my life.

Aries

19 April 2025

Dear Aries, career advancement is within reach today, and the energy supports making bold moves toward your professional goals. Whether you're seeking new responsibilities, exploring new opportunities, or expanding your skills, today's energy favors success. Stay proactive and trust in your abilities.

Affirmation & Gratitude

I trust in my skills and dedication, knowing they will lead to career success and long-term fulfillment.

Aries

20 April 2025

Dear Aries, financial matters come into focus today, and the energy supports making responsible decisions that align with your long-term financial goals. Whether you're saving for future investments, reassessing your budget, or preparing for a major purchase, today's energy favors responsible financial choices.

Affirmation & Gratitude

I make responsible financial decisions that ensure peace, stability, and security in my future.

Aries

21 April 2025

Dear Aries, creativity flows effortlessly today, making it a great time to explore new ideas and express your vision. Whether you're working on personal projects, solving challenges, or pursuing artistic endeavors, today's energy supports bold, imaginative thinking. Let your creativity guide you.

Affirmation & Gratitude

I trust in my creativity, knowing that bold ideas will lead to exciting breakthroughs and fulfilling outcomes.

Aries

22 April 2025

Dear Aries, relationships take focus today, and the energy supports nurturing deeper emotional connections with loved ones. Whether you're reconnecting with family or spending time with friends, meaningful conversations will strengthen your relationships. Be open and empathetic in your interactions.

Affirmation & Gratitude

I nurture my relationships with love, honesty, and empathy, creating deeper emotional bonds with those who bring joy into my life.

Aries

23 April 2025

Dear Aries, career progress is in the spotlight today, and the cosmos supports making bold moves toward your professional aspirations. Whether you're seeking new responsibilities or exploring new opportunities, today's energy favors proactive action. Stay confident in your abilities and take steps toward success.

Affirmation & Gratitude

I trust in my skills and dedication, knowing they will lead to career success and long-term growth.

Aries

24 April 2025

Dear Aries, financial planning is in focus today, and the energy supports making responsible decisions that align with your long-term goals. Whether you're reassessing your budget or preparing for future investments, thoughtful financial planning will bring peace and stability. Focus on long-term security.

Affirmation & Gratitude

I make thoughtful financial decisions that ensure peace, stability, and security in my future.

Aries

25 April 2025

Dear Aries, creativity is heightened today, making it a great time to explore new ideas and express your vision. Whether you're working on personal projects, solving challenges, or pursuing artistic endeavors, today's energy supports bold, imaginative thinking. Let your creativity flow freely.

Affirmation & Gratitude

I trust in my creativity, knowing that bold ideas will lead to exciting breakthroughs and fulfilling outcomes.

Aries

26 April 2025

Dear Aries, relationships take priority today, and the energy supports deepening emotional connections with loved ones. Whether you're reconnecting with family, nurturing friendships, or focusing on a romantic bond, meaningful conversations will strengthen your relationships. Be open and empathetic.

Affirmation & Gratitude

I nurture my relationships with love, honesty, and gratitude, creating deeper emotional connections with those who bring joy into my life.

Aries

27 April 2025

Dear Aries, career advancement is highlighted today, and the cosmos encourages you to take bold steps toward your professional goals. Whether you're seeking new responsibilities or expanding your skills, today's energy favors proactive action. Stay focused and confident in your abilities.

Affirmation & Gratitude

I trust in my skills and dedication, knowing they will lead to career success and long-term fulfillment.

Aries

28 April 2025

Dear Aries, financial matters come into focus today, and the energy supports making responsible decisions that align with your long-term financial goals. Whether you're saving for future investments, reassessing your budget, or preparing for a significant purchase, thoughtful financial choices will bring peace and security.

Affirmation & Gratitude

I make responsible financial decisions that ensure peace, stability, and security in my future.

Aries

29 April 2025

Dear Aries, creativity is heightened today, making it the perfect time to explore new ideas and express your vision. Whether you're working on personal projects, artistic endeavors, or solving challenges, today's energy supports bold, imaginative thinking. Let your creativity flow freely.

Affirmation & Gratitude

I trust in my creativity, knowing that bold ideas will lead to exciting breakthroughs and fulfilling outcomes.

Aries

30 April 2025

Dear Aries, relationships take focus today, and the cosmos encourages you to nurture emotional connections with loved ones. Whether you're reconnecting with family or focusing on friends, meaningful conversations will strengthen your bonds. Be open, honest, and empathetic.

Affirmation & Gratitude

I nurture my relationships with love, honesty, and gratitude, creating deeper emotional connections with those who bring joy into my life.

May

2025

Aries

1 May 2025

Dear Aries, creativity takes the spotlight today, making it a perfect time to explore new ideas and express your vision. Whether you're working on personal projects or solving challenges, today's energy supports bold, imaginative thinking. Trust in your creative abilities to bring exciting breakthroughs.

Affirmation & Gratitude

I trust in my creativity, knowing that bold ideas will lead to exciting opportunities and fulfilling outcomes.

Aries

2 May 2025

Dear Aries, relationships take priority today, and the cosmos supports deepening emotional connections with loved ones. Whether you're reconnecting with family or spending time with friends, meaningful conversations will bring you closer to those who matter most. Be open, empathetic, and honest in your interactions.

Affirmation & Gratitude

I nurture my relationships with love, honesty, and empathy, creating deeper emotional bonds with those who bring joy into my life.

Aries

3 May 2025

Dear Aries, career growth is highlighted today, and the energy encourages you to take bold steps toward your professional aspirations. Whether you're expanding your responsibilities, seeking new opportunities, or advancing in your current role, today's energy favors proactive action. Stay confident in your abilities.

Affirmation & Gratitude

I trust in my skills and hard work, knowing they will lead to career success and fulfillment.

Aries

4 May 2025

Dear Aries, financial planning takes center stage today, and the cosmos supports making responsible decisions that align with your long-term goals. Whether you're reassessing your budget or saving for future investments, thoughtful financial choices today will bring peace and stability.

Affirmation & Gratitude

I make responsible financial decisions that ensure peace, stability, and security in my future.

Aries

5 May 2025

Dear Aries, creativity flows effortlessly today, making it an ideal time to explore new ideas and bring your vision to life. Whether you're working on personal projects, artistic endeavors, or solving challenges, today's energy supports bold, imaginative thinking. Let your creativity guide you.

Affirmation & Gratitude

I trust in my creativity, knowing that bold ideas will lead to exciting breakthroughs and fulfilling outcomes.

Aries

6 May 2025

Dear Aries, relationships take focus today, and the energy supports nurturing deeper emotional connections with loved ones. Whether you're reconnecting with family or focusing on a romantic bond, meaningful conversations will strengthen your relationships. Be present, listen with empathy, and share your feelings openly.

Affirmation & Gratitude

I nurture my relationships with love, honesty, and gratitude, creating deeper emotional bonds with those who bring joy into my life.

Aries

7 May 2025

Dear Aries, career advancement is within reach today, and the cosmos supports making bold moves toward your professional goals. Whether you're seeking new responsibilities or expanding your skills, today's energy favors success. Stay proactive and confident in your abilities.

Affirmation & Gratitude

I trust in my skills and dedication, knowing they will lead to career success and long-term fulfillment.

Aries

8 May 2025

Dear Aries, financial matters come into focus today, and the energy supports making responsible decisions that align with your long-term financial goals. Whether you're reassessing your budget, saving for future investments, or preparing for a significant purchase, today's energy favors responsible financial planning.

Affirmation & Gratitude

I make responsible financial decisions that ensure peace, stability, and security in my future.

Aries

9 May 2025

Dear Aries, creativity is heightened today, making it a perfect time to explore new ideas and express your vision. Whether you're working on personal projects, artistic endeavors, or solving challenges, today's energy supports bold, imaginative thinking. Let your creativity flow freely.

Affirmation & Gratitude

I trust in my creativity, knowing that bold ideas will lead to exciting breakthroughs and fulfilling outcomes.

Aries

10 May 2025

Dear Aries, relationships take focus today, and the energy supports deepening emotional connections with loved ones. Whether you're spending time with family, friends, or a romantic partner, meaningful conversations will strengthen your relationships. Be open, honest, and empathetic in your interactions.

Affirmation & Gratitude

I nurture my relationships with love, honesty, and empathy, creating deeper emotional bonds with those who bring joy into my life.

Aries

11 May 2025

Dear Aries, career growth is in the spotlight today, and the energy supports making bold moves toward your professional goals. Whether you're seeking a promotion, expanding your responsibilities, or exploring new opportunities, today's energy favors proactive action. Stay focused on your aspirations.

Affirmation & Gratitude

I trust in my skills and dedication, knowing they will lead to career success and long-term fulfillment.

Aries

12 May 2025

Dear Aries, financial planning takes priority today, and the cosmos encourages you to make responsible decisions about your future. Whether you're reassessing your savings or preparing for a significant purchase, today's energy supports thoughtful choices that will bring peace and stability.

Affirmation & Gratitude

I make thoughtful financial decisions that ensure peace, stability, and security in my future.

Aries

13 May 2025

Dear Aries, creativity flows effortlessly today, making it a great time to explore new ideas and bring your vision to life. Whether you're working on personal projects, solving challenges, or pursuing artistic endeavors, today's energy supports bold, imaginative thinking. Let your creativity guide you.

Affirmation & Gratitude

I trust in my creativity, knowing that bold ideas will lead to exciting breakthroughs and fulfilling outcomes.

Aries

14 May 2025

Dear Aries, relationships take focus today, and the energy supports building stronger emotional connections with loved ones. Whether you're reconnecting with family, nurturing friendships, or focusing on a romantic bond, meaningful conversations will strengthen your relationships. Be open, honest, and empathetic in your interactions.

Affirmation & Gratitude

I nurture my relationships with love, honesty, and empathy, creating deeper emotional connections with those who bring joy into my life.

Aries

15 May 2025

Dear Aries, career progress is in the spotlight today, and the energy supports making bold moves toward your professional goals. Whether you're seeking a promotion, expanding your responsibilities, or exploring new opportunities, today's energy favors proactive action. Stay confident in your abilities and trust your dedication.

Affirmation & Gratitude

I trust in my hard work and skills, knowing they will lead to career success and personal fulfillment.

Aries

16 May 2025

Dear Aries, financial matters take center stage today, and the cosmos supports making responsible decisions about your future. Whether you're reassessing your budget or saving for future investments, thoughtful financial planning today will bring peace and stability.

Affirmation & Gratitude

I make responsible financial decisions that ensure peace, stability, and security in my future.

Aries

17 May 2025

Dear Aries, creativity is heightened today, making it a perfect time to explore new ideas and express your vision. Whether you're working on personal projects, solving challenges, or pursuing artistic endeavors, today's energy supports bold, imaginative thinking. Let your creativity flow freely.

Affirmation & Gratitude

I trust in my creativity, knowing that bold ideas will lead to exciting breakthroughs and fulfilling outcomes.

Aries

18 May 2025

Dear Aries, relationships take priority today, and the energy supports deepening emotional connections with loved ones. Whether you're reconnecting with family, nurturing friendships, or focusing on a romantic bond, meaningful conversations will strengthen your relationships. Be present and listen with empathy.

Affirmation & Gratitude

I nurture my relationships with love, honesty, and gratitude, creating deeper emotional connections with those who bring joy into my life.

Aries

19 May 2025

Dear Aries, career advancement is highlighted today, and the cosmos supports making bold moves toward your professional goals. Whether you're seeking new responsibilities, expanding your skills, or exploring new opportunities, today's energy favors proactive action. Stay confident and proactive.

Affirmation & Gratitude

I trust in my skills and dedication, knowing they will lead to career success and long-term fulfillment.

Aries

20 May 2025

Dear Aries, financial matters come into focus today, and the energy supports making responsible decisions that align with your long-term financial goals. Whether you're saving for future investments, reassessing your budget, or preparing for a significant purchase, thoughtful financial planning today will bring peace and security.

Affirmation & Gratitude

I make responsible financial decisions that ensure peace, stability, and security in my future.

Aries

21 May 2025

Dear Aries, creativity is heightened today, making it a great time to explore new ideas and express your vision. Whether you're working on personal projects, solving challenges, or pursuing artistic endeavors, today's energy supports bold, imaginative thinking. Let your creativity guide you.

Affirmation & Gratitude

I trust in my creativity, knowing that bold ideas will lead to exciting breakthroughs and fulfilling outcomes.

Aries

22 May 2025

Dear Aries, relationships take focus today, and the cosmos encourages you to nurture emotional connections with loved ones. Whether you're reconnecting with family, nurturing friendships, or focusing on a romantic bond, meaningful conversations will strengthen your relationships. Be open, honest, and empathetic.

Affirmation & Gratitude

I nurture my relationships with love, honesty, and empathy, creating deeper emotional connections with those who bring joy into my life.

Aries

23 May 2025

Dear Aries, career progress is in the spotlight today, and the energy supports making bold moves toward your professional goals. Whether you're seeking new responsibilities or exploring new opportunities, today's energy favors proactive action. Stay confident in your abilities and trust your dedication.

Affirmation & Gratitude

I trust in my hard work and dedication, knowing they will lead to career success and personal fulfillment.

Aries

24 May 2025

Dear Aries, financial planning is in focus today, and the energy supports making responsible decisions that align with your long-term financial goals. Whether you're reassessing your budget or preparing for future investments, thoughtful financial planning will bring peace and stability.

Affirmation & Gratitude

I make thoughtful financial decisions that ensure peace, stability, and security in my future.

Aries

25 May 2025

Dear Aries, creativity is heightened today, making it a great time to explore new ideas and express your vision. Whether you're working on personal projects, artistic endeavors, or solving challenges, today's energy supports bold, imaginative thinking. Let your creativity flow freely.

Affirmation & Gratitude

I trust in my creativity, knowing that bold ideas will lead to exciting breakthroughs and fulfilling outcomes.

Aries

26 May 2025

Dear Aries, relationships take focus today, and the cosmos encourages you to nurture emotional connections with loved ones. Whether you're reconnecting with family or focusing on friends, meaningful conversations will strengthen your bonds. Be open, honest, and empathetic.

Affirmation & Gratitude

I nurture my relationships with love, honesty, and gratitude, creating deeper emotional connections with those who bring joy into my life.

Aries

27 May 2025

Dear Aries, career growth is highlighted today, and the cosmos encourages you to take bold steps toward your professional aspirations. Whether you're seeking new responsibilities, expanding your skills, or exploring new opportunities, today's energy favors proactive action. Stay confident in your abilities.

Affirmation & Gratitude

I trust in my skills and dedication, knowing they will lead to career success and long-term growth.

Aries

28 May 2025

Dear Aries, financial matters come into focus today, and the energy supports making responsible decisions that align with your long-term financial goals. Whether you're saving for future investments, reassessing your budget, or preparing for a significant purchase, today's energy favors responsible financial planning.

Affirmation & Gratitude

I make responsible financial decisions that ensure peace, stability, and security in my future.

Aries

29 May 2025

Dear Aries, creativity is heightened today, making it a great time to explore new ideas and express your vision. Whether you're working on personal projects, artistic endeavors, or solving challenges, today's energy supports bold, imaginative thinking. Let your creativity flow freely.

Affirmation & Gratitude

I trust in my creativity, knowing that bold ideas will lead to exciting breakthroughs and fulfilling outcomes.

Aries

30 May 2025

Dear Aries, relationships take priority today, and the cosmos encourages you to nurture emotional connections with loved ones. Whether you're reconnecting with family or focusing on friends, meaningful conversations will strengthen your bonds. Be open, honest, and empathetic.

Affirmation & Gratitude

I nurture my relationships with love, honesty, and gratitude, creating deeper emotional connections with those who bring joy into my life.

Aries
31 May 2025

Dear Aries, career growth is in the spotlight today, and the energy supports making bold moves toward your professional aspirations. Whether you're seeking new responsibilities, expanding your skills, or exploring new opportunities, today's energy favors proactive action. Stay confident in your abilities and take steps toward success.

Affirmation & Gratitude

I trust in my skills and dedication, knowing they will lead to career success and fulfillment.

June

2025

Aries

1 June 2025

Dear Aries, creativity takes center stage today, making it a perfect time to explore new ideas and express your vision. Whether you're working on personal projects, artistic endeavors, or solving challenges, today's energy supports bold, imaginative thinking. Trust your instincts and allow your creativity to guide you toward exciting breakthroughs.

Affirmation & Gratitude

I trust in my creativity, knowing that bold ideas will lead to exciting opportunities and fulfilling outcomes.

Aries

2 June 2025

Dear Aries, relationships take priority today, and the cosmos encourages you to deepen emotional connections with loved ones. Whether you're spending time with family, friends, or a romantic partner, meaningful conversations will strengthen your bonds. Be open, honest, and empathetic in your interactions.

Affirmation & Gratitude

I nurture my relationships with love, honesty, and empathy, creating deeper emotional connections with those who bring joy into my life.

Aries

3 June 2025

Dear Aries, career growth is in the spotlight today, and the energy supports making bold moves toward your professional goals. Whether you're expanding your responsibilities, seeking a promotion, or exploring new opportunities, today's energy favors proactive action. Stay confident in your abilities and take decisive steps toward success.

Affirmation & Gratitude

I trust in my hard work and dedication, knowing they will lead to career success and personal fulfillment.

Aries

4 June 2025

Dear Aries, financial planning takes priority today, and the cosmos encourages you to make responsible decisions that align with your long-term financial goals. Whether you're reassessing your budget or preparing for a significant purchase, thoughtful financial planning will bring peace and stability.

Affirmation & Gratitude

I make responsible financial decisions that ensure peace, stability, and security in my future.

Aries

5 June 2025

Dear Aries, creativity flows effortlessly today, making it the perfect time to explore new ideas and bring your vision to life. Whether you're working on personal projects, solving challenges, or pursuing artistic endeavors, today's energy supports bold, imaginative thinking. Let your creativity guide you toward success.

Affirmation & Gratitude

I trust in my creativity, knowing that bold ideas will lead to exciting breakthroughs and fulfilling outcomes.

Aries

6 June 2025

Dear Aries, relationships take focus today, and the energy supports nurturing deeper emotional connections with loved ones. Whether you're reconnecting with family, spending time with friends, or focusing on a romantic bond, meaningful conversations will strengthen your relationships. Be present, listen with empathy, and share your thoughts openly.

Affirmation & Gratitude

I nurture my relationships with love, empathy, and gratitude, creating deeper emotional bonds with those who bring joy into my life.

Aries

7 June 2025

Dear Aries, career advancement is within reach today, and the energy supports making bold moves toward your professional goals. Whether you're seeking new responsibilities, exploring opportunities, or expanding your skills, today's energy favors proactive action. Stay confident and proactive in your approach.

Affirmation & Gratitude

I trust in my skills and dedication, knowing they will lead to career success and long-term fulfillment.

Aries

8 June 2025

Dear Aries, financial matters come into focus today, and the cosmos supports making responsible decisions that align with your long-term financial goals. Whether you're reassessing your budget, saving for future investments, or preparing for a major purchase, thoughtful financial planning today will bring peace and stability.

Affirmation & Gratitude

I make responsible financial decisions that ensure peace, stability, and security in my future.

Aries

9 June 2025

Dear Aries, creativity is heightened today, making it a great time to explore new ideas and bring your vision to life. Whether you're working on personal projects, solving challenges, or pursuing artistic endeavors, today's energy supports bold, imaginative thinking. Trust your creative instincts and let your creativity guide you toward exciting breakthroughs.

Affirmation & Gratitude

I trust in my creativity, knowing that bold ideas will lead to exciting breakthroughs and fulfilling outcomes.

Aries

10 June 2025

Dear Aries, relationships take priority today, and the cosmos encourages you to nurture deeper emotional connections with loved ones. Whether you're reconnecting with family, friends, or focusing on a romantic bond, meaningful conversations will strengthen your relationships. Be open, honest, and empathetic in your interactions.

Affirmation & Gratitude

I nurture my relationships with love, honesty, and gratitude, creating deeper emotional bonds with those who bring joy into my life.

Aries

11 June 2025

Dear Aries, career growth is in the spotlight today, and the energy supports making bold moves toward your professional goals. Whether you're seeking new opportunities, expanding your responsibilities, or honing your skills, today's energy favors proactive action. Stay confident in your abilities and take steps toward success.

Affirmation & Gratitude

I trust in my skills and dedication, knowing they will lead to career success and personal fulfillment.

Aries

12 June 2025

Dear Aries, financial planning takes priority today, and the cosmos supports making responsible decisions about your future. Whether you're reassessing your savings or preparing for future investments, today's energy favors thoughtful choices that will bring peace and stability.

Affirmation & Gratitude

I make thoughtful financial decisions that ensure peace, stability, and security in my future.

Aries

13 June 2025

Dear Aries, creativity flows effortlessly today, making it a great time to explore new ideas and express your vision. Whether you're working on personal projects, solving challenges, or pursuing artistic endeavors, today's energy supports bold, imaginative thinking. Let your creativity guide you.

Affirmation & Gratitude

I trust in my creativity, knowing that bold ideas will lead to exciting breakthroughs and fulfilling outcomes.

Aries

14 June 2025

Dear Aries, relationships take focus today, and the energy supports nurturing deeper emotional connections with loved ones. Whether you're reconnecting with family or spending time with friends, meaningful conversations will strengthen your bonds. Be open, honest, and empathetic.

Affirmation & Gratitude

I nurture my relationships with love, honesty, and gratitude, creating deeper emotional bonds with those who bring joy into my life.

Aries

15 June 2025

Dear Aries, career progress is in the spotlight today, and the cosmos supports making bold moves toward your professional goals. Whether you're seeking a promotion, expanding your responsibilities, or exploring new opportunities, today's energy favors proactive action. Stay confident in your abilities and trust your dedication.

Affirmation & Gratitude

I trust in my hard work and skills, knowing they will lead to career success and personal fulfillment.

Aries

16 June 2025

Dear Aries, financial matters take center stage today, and the energy supports making responsible decisions that align with your long-term financial goals. Whether you're reassessing your budget or preparing for future investments, thoughtful financial planning today will bring peace and stability. Focus on long-term security.

Affirmation & Gratitude

I make responsible financial decisions that ensure peace, stability, and security in my future.

Aries

17 June 2025

Dear Aries, creativity is heightened today, making it a great time to explore new ideas and express your vision. Whether you're working on personal projects, solving challenges, or pursuing artistic endeavors, today's energy supports bold, imaginative thinking. Let your creativity flow freely.

Affirmation & Gratitude

I trust in my creativity, knowing that bold ideas will lead to exciting breakthroughs and fulfilling outcomes.

Aries

18 June 2025

Dear Aries, relationships take priority today, and the energy supports deepening emotional connections with loved ones. Whether you're reconnecting with family, nurturing friendships, or focusing on a romantic bond, meaningful conversations will strengthen your relationships. Be present, listen with empathy, and share your thoughts openly.

Affirmation & Gratitude

I nurture my relationships with love, honesty, and gratitude, creating deeper emotional connections with those who bring joy into my life.

Aries

19 June 2025

Dear Aries, career advancement is within reach today, and the energy supports making bold moves toward your professional goals. Whether you're seeking new responsibilities, expanding your skills, or exploring new opportunities, today's energy favors success. Stay confident and proactive.

Affirmation & Gratitude

I trust in my skills and dedication, knowing they will lead to career success and long-term fulfillment.

Aries

20 June 2025

Dear Aries, financial matters come into focus today, and the energy supports making responsible decisions that align with your long-term financial goals. Whether you're saving for future investments, reassessing your budget, or preparing for a major purchase, today's energy favors responsible financial planning.

Affirmation & Gratitude

I make responsible financial decisions that ensure peace, stability, and security in my future.

Aries

21 June 2025

Dear Aries, creativity is heightened today, making it a great time to explore new ideas and bring your vision to life. Whether you're working on personal projects, solving challenges, or pursuing artistic endeavors, today's energy supports bold, imaginative thinking. Let your creativity guide you.

Affirmation & Gratitude

I trust in my creativity, knowing that bold ideas will lead to exciting breakthroughs and fulfilling outcomes.

Aries

22 June 2025

Dear Aries, relationships take priority today, and the cosmos encourages you to nurture emotional connections with loved ones. Whether you're reconnecting with family or focusing on friends, meaningful conversations will strengthen your bonds. Be open, honest, and empathetic.

Affirmation & Gratitude

I nurture my relationships with love, honesty, and gratitude, creating deeper emotional connections with those who bring joy into my life.

Aries

23 June 2025

Dear Aries, career progress is highlighted today, and the energy supports making bold moves toward your professional goals. Whether you're seeking new responsibilities or exploring new opportunities, today's energy favors proactive action. Stay confident in your abilities and trust your dedication.

Affirmation & Gratitude

I trust in my hard work and dedication, knowing they will lead to career success and personal fulfillment.

Aries

24 June 2025

Dear Aries, financial planning is in focus today, and the energy supports making responsible decisions that align with your long-term financial goals. Whether you're reassessing your budget or preparing for future investments, thoughtful financial planning will bring peace and stability. Focus on long-term security.

Affirmation & Gratitude

I make thoughtful financial decisions that ensure peace, stability, and security in my future.

Aries

25 June 2025

Dear Aries, creativity flows effortlessly today, making it a great time to explore new ideas and express your vision. Whether you're working on personal projects, solving challenges, or pursuing artistic endeavors, today's energy supports bold, imaginative thinking. Let your creativity guide you toward success.

Affirmation & Gratitude

I trust in my creativity, knowing that bold ideas will lead to exciting breakthroughs and fulfilling outcomes.

Aries

26 June 2025

Dear Aries, relationships take priority today, and the energy supports building deeper emotional connections with loved ones. Whether you're reconnecting with family or nurturing friendships, meaningful conversations will strengthen your relationships. Be open and empathetic in your interactions.

Affirmation & Gratitude

I nurture my relationships with love, honesty, and empathy, creating deeper emotional bonds with those who bring joy into my life.

Aries

27 June 2025

Dear Aries, career advancement is highlighted today, and the cosmos encourages you to take bold steps toward your professional goals. Whether you're seeking a promotion or expanding your responsibilities, today's energy favors proactive action. Stay focused and confident in your abilities.

Affirmation & Gratitude

I trust in my skills and dedication, knowing they will lead to career success and long-term fulfillment.

Aries

28 June 2025

Dear Aries, financial matters come into focus today, and the energy supports making responsible decisions that align with your long-term financial goals. Whether you're saving for future investments, reassessing your budget, or preparing for a significant purchase, thoughtful financial planning will bring peace and security.

Affirmation & Gratitude

I make responsible financial decisions that ensure peace, stability, and security in my future.

Aries

29 June 2025

Dear Aries, creativity is heightened today, making it the perfect time to explore new ideas and express your vision. Whether you're working on personal projects, artistic endeavors, or solving challenges, today's energy supports bold, imaginative thinking. Let your creativity flow freely.

Affirmation & Gratitude

I trust in my creativity, knowing that bold ideas will lead to exciting breakthroughs and fulfilling outcomes.

Aries

30 June 2025

Dear Aries, relationships take focus today, and the cosmos encourages you to nurture emotional connections with loved ones. Whether you're reconnecting with family or focusing on friends, meaningful conversations will strengthen your bonds. Be open, honest, and empathetic.

Affirmation & Gratitude

I nurture my relationships with love, honesty, and gratitude, creating deeper emotional connections with those who bring joy into my life.

July

2025

Aries

1 July 2025

Dear Aries, creativity takes the spotlight today, making it a perfect time to explore new ideas and express your vision. Whether you're working on personal projects or artistic endeavors, today's energy supports bold, imaginative thinking. Trust your instincts and let your creativity guide you toward exciting breakthroughs.

Affirmation & Gratitude

I trust in my creativity, knowing that bold ideas will lead to exciting opportunities and fulfilling outcomes.

Aries

2 July 2025

Dear Aries, relationships take priority today, and the cosmos encourages you to nurture emotional connections with loved ones. Whether you're reconnecting with family, friends, or a romantic partner, meaningful conversations will strengthen your bonds. Be open, honest, and empathetic in your interactions.

Affirmation & Gratitude

I nurture my relationships with love, honesty, and empathy, creating deeper emotional connections with those who bring joy into my life.

Aries

3 July 2025

Dear Aries, career growth is highlighted today, and the energy supports making bold moves toward your professional goals. Whether you're seeking a promotion, expanding your responsibilities, or exploring new opportunities, today's energy favors proactive action. Stay confident in your abilities and take decisive steps toward success.

Affirmation & Gratitude

I trust in my hard work and dedication, knowing they will lead to career success and personal fulfillment.

Aries

4 July 2025

Dear Aries, financial planning takes priority today, and the cosmos encourages you to make responsible decisions that align with your long-term financial goals. Whether you're reassessing your budget or preparing for a significant purchase, thoughtful financial planning today will bring peace and stability.

Affirmation & Gratitude

I make responsible financial decisions that ensure peace, stability, and security in my future.

Aries

5 July 2025

Dear Aries, creativity flows effortlessly today, making it the perfect time to explore new ideas and bring your vision to life. Whether you're working on personal projects, solving challenges, or pursuing artistic endeavors, today's energy supports bold, imaginative thinking. Let your creativity guide you toward success.

Affirmation & Gratitude

I trust in my creativity, knowing that bold ideas will lead to exciting breakthroughs and fulfilling outcomes.

Aries

6 July 2025

Dear Aries, relationships take focus today, and the energy supports nurturing deeper emotional connections with loved ones. Whether you're reconnecting with family, friends, or a romantic partner, meaningful conversations will strengthen your relationships. Be present, listen with empathy, and share your thoughts openly.

Affirmation & Gratitude

I nurture my relationships with love, honesty, and empathy, creating deeper emotional connections with those who bring joy into my life.

Aries

7 July 2025

Dear Aries, career advancement is within reach today, and the energy supports making bold moves toward your professional goals. Whether you're seeking new responsibilities, exploring opportunities, or expanding your skills, today's energy favors proactive action. Stay confident and proactive in your approach.

Affirmation & Gratitude

I trust in my skills and dedication, knowing they will lead to career success and long-term fulfillment.

Aries

8 July 2025

Dear Aries, financial matters come into focus today, and the cosmos supports making responsible decisions that align with your long-term financial goals. Whether you're reassessing your budget, saving for future investments, or preparing for a major purchase, thoughtful financial planning today will bring peace and stability.

Affirmation & Gratitude

I make responsible financial decisions that ensure peace, stability, and security in my future.

Aries

9 July 2025

Dear Aries, creativity is heightened today, making it a great time to explore new ideas and bring your vision to life. Whether you're working on personal projects, solving challenges, or pursuing artistic endeavors, today's energy supports bold, imaginative thinking. Trust your creative instincts and let your creativity guide you toward exciting breakthroughs.

Affirmation & Gratitude

I trust in my creativity, knowing that bold ideas will lead to exciting breakthroughs and fulfilling outcomes.

Aries

10 July 2025

Dear Aries, relationships take priority today, and the cosmos encourages you to nurture deeper emotional connections with loved ones. Whether you're reconnecting with family, friends, or focusing on a romantic bond, meaningful conversations will strengthen your relationships. Be open, honest, and empathetic in your interactions.

Affirmation & Gratitude

I nurture my relationships with love, honesty, and gratitude, creating deeper emotional connections with those who bring joy into my life.

Aries

11 July 2025

Dear Aries, career growth is in the spotlight today, and the energy supports making bold moves toward your professional goals. Whether you're seeking new opportunities, expanding your responsibilities, or honing your skills, today's energy favors proactive action. Stay confident in your abilities and take steps toward success.

Affirmation & Gratitude

I trust in my skills and dedication, knowing they will lead to career success and personal fulfillment.

Aries

12 July 2025

Dear Aries, financial planning takes priority today, and the cosmos supports making responsible decisions that align with your long-term financial goals. Whether you're reassessing your budget or preparing for future investments, today's energy favors thoughtful choices that will bring peace and stability.

Affirmation & Gratitude

I make thoughtful financial decisions that ensure peace, stability, and security in my future.

Aries

13 July 2025

Dear Aries, creativity flows effortlessly today, making it a great time to explore new ideas and bring your vision to life. Whether you're working on personal projects, solving challenges, or pursuing artistic endeavors, today's energy supports bold, imaginative thinking. Let your creativity guide you.

Affirmation & Gratitude

I trust in my creativity, knowing that bold ideas will lead to exciting breakthroughs and fulfilling outcomes.

Aries

14 July 2025

Dear Aries, relationships take focus today, and the energy supports nurturing deeper emotional connections with loved ones. Whether you're reconnecting with family or focusing on friendships, meaningful conversations will strengthen your relationships. Be open, honest, and empathetic in your interactions.

Affirmation & Gratitude

I nurture my relationships with love, honesty, and gratitude, creating deeper emotional connections with those who bring joy into my life.

Aries

15 July 2025

Dear Aries, career progress is highlighted today, and the cosmos supports making bold moves toward your professional goals. Whether you're seeking a promotion, expanding your responsibilities, or exploring new opportunities, today's energy favors proactive action. Stay confident in your abilities and trust your dedication.

Affirmation & Gratitude

I trust in my hard work and skills, knowing they will lead to career success and personal fulfillment.

Aries

16 July 2025

Dear Aries, financial matters take center stage today, and the energy supports making responsible decisions that align with your long-term financial goals. Whether you're reassessing your budget or preparing for future investments, thoughtful financial planning today will bring peace and stability. Focus on long-term security.

Affirmation & Gratitude

I make responsible financial decisions that ensure peace, stability, and security in my future.

Aries

17 July 2025

Dear Aries, creativity is heightened today, making it the perfect time to explore new ideas and express your vision. Whether you're working on personal projects, solving challenges, or pursuing artistic endeavors, today's energy supports bold, imaginative thinking. Let your creativity flow freely.

Affirmation & Gratitude

I trust in my creativity, knowing that bold ideas will lead to exciting breakthroughs and fulfilling outcomes.

Aries

18 July 2025

Dear Aries, relationships take priority today, and the cosmos encourages you to nurture emotional connections with loved ones. Whether you're reconnecting with family or focusing on a romantic bond, meaningful conversations will strengthen your relationships. Be present and listen with empathy.

Affirmation & Gratitude

I nurture my relationships with love, honesty, and gratitude, creating deeper emotional bonds with those who bring joy into my life.

Aries

19 July 2025

Dear Aries, career advancement is within reach today, and the energy supports making bold moves toward your professional goals. Whether you're seeking new responsibilities, expanding your skills, or exploring new opportunities, today's energy favors success. Stay proactive and confident in your approach.

Affirmation & Gratitude

I trust in my skills and dedication, knowing they will lead to career success and long-term fulfillment.

Aries

20 July 2025

Dear Aries, financial matters come into focus today, and the cosmos encourages you to make responsible decisions that align with your long-term financial goals. Whether you're saving for future investments, reassessing your budget, or preparing for a significant purchase, thoughtful financial planning today will bring peace and security.

Affirmation & Gratitude

I make responsible financial decisions that ensure peace, stability, and security in my future.

Aries

21 July 2025

Dear Aries, creativity is heightened today, making it a perfect time to explore new ideas and express your vision. Whether you're working on personal projects, artistic endeavors, or solving challenges, today's energy supports bold, imaginative thinking. Let your creativity guide you.

Affirmation & Gratitude

I trust in my creativity, knowing that bold ideas will lead to exciting breakthroughs and fulfilling outcomes.

Aries

22 July 2025

Dear Aries, relationships take focus today, and the cosmos supports nurturing emotional connections with loved ones. Whether you're reconnecting with family or focusing on friendships, meaningful conversations will strengthen your bonds. Be open, honest, and empathetic.

Affirmation & Gratitude

I nurture my relationships with love, honesty, and gratitude, creating deeper emotional connections with those who bring joy into my life.

Aries

23 July 2025

Dear Aries, career progress is in the spotlight today, and the energy supports making bold moves toward your professional goals. Whether you're seeking new responsibilities or exploring new opportunities, today's energy favors proactive action. Stay confident in your abilities and trust your dedication.

Affirmation & Gratitude

I trust in my hard work and dedication, knowing they will lead to career success and personal fulfillment.

Aries

24 July 2025

Dear Aries, financial planning is in focus today, and the cosmos encourages you to make responsible decisions that align with your long-term financial goals. Whether you're reassessing your budget or preparing for future investments, thoughtful financial planning will bring peace and stability. Focus on long-term security.

Affirmation & Gratitude

I make responsible financial decisions that ensure peace, stability, and security in my future.

Aries

25 July 2025

Dear Aries, creativity flows effortlessly today, making it a great time to explore new ideas and express your vision. Whether you're working on personal projects, solving challenges, or pursuing artistic endeavors, today's energy supports bold, imaginative thinking. Let your creativity guide you toward success.

Affirmation & Gratitude

I trust in my creativity, knowing that bold ideas will lead to exciting breakthroughs and fulfilling outcomes.

Aries

26 July 2025

Dear Aries, relationships take priority today, and the cosmos encourages you to nurture emotional connections with loved ones. Whether you're reconnecting with family or focusing on friends, meaningful conversations will strengthen your bonds. Be open, honest, and empathetic.

Affirmation & Gratitude

I nurture my relationships with love, honesty, and empathy, creating deeper emotional bonds with those who bring joy into my life.

Aries

27 July 2025

Dear Aries, career advancement is highlighted today, and the energy supports making bold moves toward your professional goals. Whether you're seeking new responsibilities, expanding your skills, or exploring new opportunities, today's energy favors proactive action. Stay focused and confident in your abilities.

Affirmation & Gratitude

I trust in my skills and dedication, knowing they will lead to career success and long-term fulfillment.

Aries

28 July 2025

Dear Aries, financial matters come into focus today, and the cosmos encourages you to make responsible decisions that align with your long-term financial goals. Whether you're saving for future investments, reassessing your budget, or preparing for a significant purchase, thoughtful financial planning will bring peace and security.

Affirmation & Gratitude

I make responsible financial decisions that ensure peace, stability, and security in my future.

Aries

29 July 2025

Dear Aries, creativity is heightened today, making it the perfect time to explore new ideas and express your vision. Whether you're working on personal projects, artistic endeavors, or solving challenges, today's energy supports bold, imaginative thinking. Let your creativity flow freely.

Affirmation & Gratitude

I trust in my creativity, knowing that bold ideas will lead to exciting breakthroughs and fulfilling outcomes.

Aries

30 July 2025

Dear Aries, relationships take focus today, and the cosmos encourages you to nurture emotional connections with loved ones. Whether you're reconnecting with family or focusing on friends, meaningful conversations will strengthen your bonds. Be open, honest, and empathetic.

Affirmation & Gratitude

I nurture my relationships with love, honesty, and gratitude, creating deeper emotional connections with those who bring joy into my life.

Aries

31 July 2025

Dear Aries, career growth is in the spotlight today, and the energy supports making bold moves toward your professional aspirations. Whether you're seeking new responsibilities or exploring new opportunities, today's energy favors proactive action. Stay confident in your abilities and take steps toward success.

Affirmation & Gratitude

I trust in my skills and dedication, knowing they will lead to career success and fulfillment.

August

2025

Aries

1 August 2025

Dear Aries, creativity is heightened today, making it a perfect time to explore new ideas and express your vision. Whether you're working on personal projects, artistic endeavors, or solving challenges, today's energy supports bold, imaginative thinking. Trust your creative instincts to guide you toward exciting breakthroughs.

Affirmation & Gratitude

I trust in my creativity, knowing that bold ideas will lead to exciting opportunities and fulfilling outcomes.

Aries

2 August 2025

Dear Aries, relationships take focus today, and the cosmos encourages you to deepen emotional connections with loved ones. Whether you're reconnecting with family or friends, meaningful conversations will strengthen your relationships. Be open, empathetic, and honest in your interactions.

Affirmation & Gratitude

I nurture my relationships with love, honesty, and empathy, creating deeper emotional connections with those who bring joy into my life.

Aries

3 August 2025

Dear Aries, career growth is highlighted today, and the energy supports making bold moves toward your professional aspirations. Whether you're seeking a promotion, expanding your responsibilities, or exploring new opportunities, today's energy favors proactive action. Stay confident in your abilities and take steps toward success.

Affirmation & Gratitude

I trust in my skills and hard work, knowing they will lead to career success and personal fulfillment.

Aries

4 August 2025

Dear Aries, financial planning takes priority today, and the cosmos supports making responsible decisions that align with your long-term goals. Whether you're reassessing your budget or preparing for future investments, thoughtful financial choices today will bring peace and stability.

Affirmation & Gratitude

I make responsible financial decisions that ensure peace, stability, and security in my future.

Aries

5 August 2025

Dear Aries, creativity flows effortlessly today, making it a great time to explore new ideas and bring your vision to life. Whether you're working on personal projects, solving challenges, or pursuing artistic endeavors, today's energy supports bold, imaginative thinking. Let your creativity guide you.

Affirmation & Gratitude

I trust in my creativity, knowing that bold ideas will lead to exciting breakthroughs and fulfilling outcomes.

Aries

6 August 2025

Dear Aries, relationships take priority today, and the energy supports nurturing deeper emotional connections with loved ones. Whether you're reconnecting with family, spending time with friends, or focusing on a romantic relationship, meaningful conversations will strengthen your bonds. Be present and listen with empathy.

Affirmation & Gratitude

I nurture my relationships with love, honesty, and gratitude, creating deeper emotional bonds with those who bring joy into my life.

Aries

7 August 2025

Dear Aries, career advancement is within reach today, and the energy supports making bold moves toward your professional goals. Whether you're expanding your responsibilities or seeking new opportunities, today's energy favors success. Stay proactive and confident in your abilities.

Affirmation & Gratitude

I trust in my skills and dedication, knowing they will lead to career success and long-term fulfillment.

Aries

8 August 2025

Dear Aries, financial matters come into focus today, and the energy supports making responsible decisions that align with your long-term financial goals. Whether you're reassessing your budget, saving for future investments, or preparing for a significant purchase, thoughtful financial planning today will bring peace and security.

Affirmation & Gratitude

I make responsible financial decisions that ensure peace, stability, and security in my future.

Aries

9 August 2025

Dear Aries, creativity is heightened today, making it an ideal time to explore new ideas and bring your vision to life. Whether you're working on personal projects, solving challenges, or pursuing artistic endeavors, today's energy supports bold, imaginative thinking. Trust your instincts and let your creativity guide you toward success.

Affirmation & Gratitude

I trust in my creativity, knowing that bold ideas will lead to exciting breakthroughs and fulfilling outcomes.

Aries

10 August 2025

Dear Aries, relationships take focus today, and the cosmos supports nurturing emotional connections with loved ones. Whether you're spending time with family or focusing on a romantic bond, meaningful conversations will strengthen your relationships. Be open, honest, and empathetic in your interactions.

Affirmation & Gratitude

I nurture my relationships with love, honesty, and gratitude, creating deeper emotional connections with those who bring joy into my life.

Aries

11 August 2025

Dear Aries, career growth is in the spotlight today, and the energy supports making bold moves toward your professional aspirations. Whether you're seeking a promotion, expanding your responsibilities, or exploring new opportunities, today's energy favors proactive action. Stay focused on your goals.

Affirmation & Gratitude

I trust in my skills and dedication, knowing they will lead to career success and personal fulfillment.

Aries

12 August 2025

Dear Aries, financial planning takes priority today, and the cosmos supports making responsible decisions that align with your long-term goals. Whether you're reassessing your budget or preparing for a significant purchase, thoughtful financial planning today will bring peace and stability.

Affirmation & Gratitude

I make thoughtful financial decisions that ensure peace, stability, and security in my future.

Aries

13 August 2025

Dear Aries, creativity flows freely today, making it the perfect time to explore new ideas and express your vision. Whether you're working on personal projects or artistic endeavors, today's energy supports bold, imaginative thinking. Let your creativity lead you toward exciting breakthroughs.

Affirmation & Gratitude

I trust in my creativity, knowing that bold ideas will lead to exciting opportunities and fulfilling outcomes.

Aries

14 August 2025

Dear Aries, relationships take focus today, and the energy supports nurturing deeper emotional connections with loved ones. Whether you're spending time with family, friends, or focusing on a romantic relationship, meaningful conversations will strengthen your bonds. Be present and empathetic in your interactions.

Affirmation & Gratitude

I nurture my relationships with love, honesty, and gratitude, creating deeper emotional bonds with those who bring joy into my life.

Aries

15 August 2025

Dear Aries, career advancement is highlighted today, and the cosmos encourages you to take bold steps toward your professional aspirations. Whether you're seeking a promotion, expanding your responsibilities, or exploring new opportunities, today's energy favors proactive action. Stay confident in your abilities.

Affirmation & Gratitude

I trust in my skills and hard work, knowing they will lead to career success and personal fulfillment.

Aries

16 August 2025

Dear Aries, financial matters take center stage today, and the energy supports making responsible decisions that align with your long-term financial goals. Whether you're reassessing your budget or preparing for future investments, thoughtful financial planning today will bring peace and stability.

Affirmation & Gratitude

I make responsible financial decisions that ensure peace, stability, and security in my future.

Aries

17 August 2025

Dear Aries, creativity is heightened today, making it a great time to explore new ideas and express your vision. Whether you're working on personal projects, solving challenges, or pursuing artistic endeavors, today's energy supports bold, imaginative thinking. Let your creativity flow and guide you toward success.

Affirmation & Gratitude

I trust in my creativity, knowing that bold ideas will lead to exciting breakthroughs and fulfilling outcomes.

Aries

18 August 2025

Dear Aries, relationships take priority today, and the cosmos supports building stronger emotional connections with loved ones. Whether you're reconnecting with family or nurturing friendships, meaningful conversations will deepen your bonds. Be open, honest, and empathetic in your interactions.

Affirmation & Gratitude

I nurture my relationships with love, empathy, and honesty, creating deeper emotional bonds with those who bring joy into my life.

Aries

19 August 2025

Dear Aries, career progress is in the spotlight today, and the energy supports making bold moves toward your professional goals. Whether you're seeking a promotion, expanding your responsibilities, or exploring new opportunities, today's energy favors proactive action. Stay confident and trust your abilities.

Affirmation & Gratitude

I trust in my hard work and dedication, knowing they will lead to career success and personal fulfillment.

Aries

20 August 2025

Dear Aries, financial matters take focus today, and the cosmos supports making responsible decisions that align with your long-term financial goals. Whether you're reassessing your budget or saving for future investments, thoughtful financial choices today will bring peace and stability.

Affirmation & Gratitude

I make responsible financial decisions that ensure peace, stability, and security in my future.

Aries

21 August 2025

Dear Aries, creativity is heightened today, making it an ideal time to explore new ideas and bring your vision to life. Whether you're working on personal projects or artistic endeavors, today's energy supports bold, imaginative thinking. Trust your instincts and let your creativity lead the way.

Affirmation & Gratitude

I trust in my creativity, knowing that bold ideas will lead to exciting breakthroughs and fulfilling outcomes.

Aries

22 August 2025

Dear Aries, relationships take focus today, and the cosmos encourages you to nurture emotional connections with loved ones. Whether you're reconnecting with family or spending time with friends, meaningful conversations will deepen your relationships. Be open, honest, and empathetic.

Affirmation & Gratitude

I nurture my relationships with love, honesty, and gratitude, creating deeper emotional bonds with those who bring joy into my life.

Aries

23 August 2025

Dear Aries, career growth is highlighted today, and the energy supports making bold moves toward your professional goals. Whether you're expanding your responsibilities or exploring new opportunities, today's energy favors proactive action. Stay confident in your abilities and focus on your aspirations.

Affirmation & Gratitude

I trust in my skills and dedication, knowing they will lead to career success and personal fulfillment.

Aries

24 August 2025

Dear Aries, financial planning is in focus today, and the cosmos encourages you to make responsible decisions that align with your long-term financial goals. Whether you're reassessing your budget or preparing for a significant purchase, thoughtful financial planning today will bring peace and stability.

Affirmation & Gratitude

I make responsible financial decisions that ensure peace, stability, and security in my future.

Aries

25 August 2025

Dear Aries, creativity flows effortlessly today, making it a great time to explore new ideas and express your vision. Whether you're working on personal projects, artistic endeavors, or solving challenges, today's energy supports bold, imaginative thinking. Let your creativity guide you toward success.

Affirmation & Gratitude

I trust in my creativity, knowing that bold ideas will lead to exciting breakthroughs and fulfilling outcomes.

Aries

26 August 2025

Dear Aries, relationships take priority today, and the cosmos supports building stronger emotional connections with loved ones. Whether you're reconnecting with family or focusing on a romantic bond, meaningful conversations will strengthen your relationships. Be present and empathetic in your interactions.

Affirmation & Gratitude

I nurture my relationships with love, honesty, and empathy, creating deeper emotional bonds with those who bring joy into my life.

Aries

27 August 2025

Dear Aries, career progress is highlighted today, and the cosmos encourages you to take bold steps toward your professional goals. Whether you're seeking a promotion, expanding your responsibilities, or exploring new opportunities, today's energy favors proactive action. Stay focused and confident in your abilities.

Affirmation & Gratitude

I trust in my skills and dedication, knowing they will lead to career success and long-term fulfillment.

Aries

28 August 2025

Dear Aries, financial matters take focus today, and the energy supports making responsible decisions that align with your long-term financial goals. Whether you're reassessing your budget or saving for future investments, thoughtful financial planning today will bring peace and stability.

Affirmation & Gratitude

I make responsible financial decisions that ensure peace, stability, and security in my future.

Aries

29 August 2025

Dear Aries, creativity is heightened today, making it a great time to explore new ideas and bring your vision to life. Whether you're working on personal projects or solving challenges, today's energy supports bold, imaginative thinking. Let your creativity flow freely.

Affirmation & Gratitude

I trust in my creativity, knowing that bold ideas will lead to exciting breakthroughs and fulfilling outcomes.

Aries

30 August 2025

Dear Aries, relationships take focus today, and the cosmos encourages you to nurture emotional connections with loved ones. Whether you're reconnecting with family or focusing on friendships, meaningful conversations will strengthen your bonds. Be open, honest, and empathetic.

Affirmation & Gratitude

I nurture my relationships with love, honesty, and gratitude, creating deeper emotional connections with those who bring joy into my life.

Aries

31 August 2025

Dear Aries, career growth is in the spotlight today, and the energy supports making bold moves toward your professional aspirations. Whether you're seeking new responsibilities, expanding your skills, or exploring new opportunities, today's energy favors proactive action. Stay confident in your abilities.

Affirmation & Gratitude

I trust in my skills and dedication, knowing they will lead to career success and fulfillment.

September
2025

Aries

1 September 2025

Dear Aries, creativity is in full swing today, making it a perfect time to explore new ideas and bring your vision to life. Whether you're working on personal projects, solving challenges, or pursuing artistic endeavors, today's energy supports bold, imaginative thinking. Let your creativity guide you toward exciting breakthroughs.

Affirmation & Gratitude

I trust in my creativity, knowing that bold ideas will lead to exciting opportunities and fulfilling outcomes.

Aries

2 September 2025

Dear Aries, relationships take focus today, and the cosmos encourages you to nurture emotional connections with loved ones. Whether you're spending time with family or friends, meaningful conversations will strengthen your bonds. Be open, empathetic, and honest in your interactions.

Affirmation & Gratitude

I nurture my relationships with love, honesty, and empathy, creating deeper emotional connections with those who bring joy into my life.

Aries

3 September 2025

Dear Aries, career growth is highlighted today, and the energy supports making bold moves toward your professional aspirations. Whether you're seeking a promotion, expanding your responsibilities, or exploring new opportunities, today's energy favors proactive action. Stay confident in your abilities and take decisive steps toward success.

Affirmation & Gratitude

I trust in my skills and dedication, knowing they will lead to career success and personal fulfillment.

Aries

4 September 2025

Dear Aries, financial planning takes priority today, and the cosmos encourages you to make responsible decisions that align with your long-term goals. Whether you're reassessing your budget or preparing for future investments, thoughtful financial planning today will bring peace and stability.

Affirmation & Gratitude

I make responsible financial decisions that ensure peace, stability, and security in my future.

Aries

5 September 2025

Dear Aries, creativity flows effortlessly today, making it the perfect time to explore new ideas and express your vision. Whether you're working on personal projects, solving challenges, or pursuing artistic endeavors, today's energy supports bold, imaginative thinking. Let your creativity lead you toward exciting breakthroughs.

Affirmation & Gratitude

I trust in my creativity, knowing that bold ideas will lead to exciting breakthroughs and fulfilling outcomes.

Aries

6 September 2025

Dear Aries, relationships take priority today, and the cosmos encourages you to nurture emotional connections with loved ones. Whether you're reconnecting with family or focusing on friendships, meaningful conversations will strengthen your bonds. Be open, honest, and empathetic.

Affirmation & Gratitude

I nurture my relationships with love, honesty, and gratitude, creating deeper emotional bonds with those who bring joy into my life.

Aries

7 September 2025

Dear Aries, career progress is in the spotlight today, and the energy supports making bold moves toward your professional goals. Whether you're seeking new responsibilities or exploring new opportunities, today's energy favors proactive action. Stay confident in your abilities and trust your dedication.

Affirmation & Gratitude

I trust in my hard work and dedication, knowing they will lead to career success and personal fulfillment.

Aries

8 September 2025

Dear Aries, financial matters come into focus today, and the cosmos encourages you to make responsible decisions that align with your long-term financial goals. Whether you're reassessing your budget, saving for future investments, or preparing for a significant purchase, thoughtful financial planning today will bring peace and stability.

Affirmation & Gratitude

I make responsible financial decisions that ensure peace, stability, and security in my future.

Aries

9 September 2025

Dear Aries, creativity is heightened today, making it a great time to explore new ideas and bring your vision to life. Whether you're working on personal projects or artistic endeavors, today's energy supports bold, imaginative thinking. Trust your instincts and let your creativity guide you toward success.

Affirmation & Gratitude

I trust in my creativity, knowing that bold ideas will lead to exciting breakthroughs and fulfilling outcomes.

Aries

10 September 2025

Dear Aries, relationships take focus today, and the cosmos supports nurturing emotional connections with loved ones. Whether you're reconnecting with family or focusing on friendships, meaningful conversations will deepen your bonds. Be open, honest, and empathetic in your interactions.

Affirmation & Gratitude

I nurture my relationships with love, honesty, and gratitude, creating deeper emotional connections with those who bring joy into my life.

Aries

11 September 2025

Dear Aries, career growth is in the spotlight today, and the energy supports making bold moves toward your professional aspirations. Whether you're seeking a promotion, expanding your responsibilities, or exploring new opportunities, today's energy favors proactive action. Stay confident in your abilities.

Affirmation & Gratitude

I trust in my skills and dedication, knowing they will lead to career success and personal fulfillment.

Aries

12 September 2025

Dear Aries, financial planning takes priority today, and the cosmos supports making responsible decisions that align with your long-term financial goals. Whether you're reassessing your budget or preparing for future investments, thoughtful financial choices today will bring peace and stability.

Affirmation & Gratitude

I make thoughtful financial decisions that ensure peace, stability, and security in my future.

Aries

13 September 2025

Dear Aries, creativity flows effortlessly today, making it a perfect time to explore new ideas and express your vision. Whether you're working on personal projects, solving challenges, or pursuing artistic endeavors, today's energy supports bold, imaginative thinking. Let your creativity guide you toward success.

Affirmation & Gratitude

I trust in my creativity, knowing that bold ideas will lead to exciting breakthroughs and fulfilling outcomes.

Aries

14 September 2025

Dear Aries, relationships take focus today, and the cosmos encourages you to nurture emotional connections with loved ones. Whether you're reconnecting with family, spending time with friends, or focusing on a romantic relationship, meaningful conversations will strengthen your relationships. Be present, empathetic, and open in your interactions.

Affirmation & Gratitude

I nurture my relationships with love, honesty, and gratitude, creating deeper emotional bonds with those who bring joy into my life.

Aries

15 September 2025

Dear Aries, career advancement is within reach today, and the energy supports making bold moves toward your professional goals. Whether you're seeking new responsibilities, expanding your skills, or exploring new opportunities, today's energy favors success. Stay confident and proactive in your approach.

Affirmation & Gratitude

I trust in my skills and dedication, knowing they will lead to career success and long-term fulfillment.

Aries

16 September 2025

Dear Aries, financial matters come into focus today, and the cosmos encourages you to make responsible decisions that align with your long-term financial goals. Whether you're reassessing your budget, saving for future investments, or preparing for a significant purchase, today's energy supports thoughtful financial planning.

Affirmation & Gratitude

I make responsible financial decisions that ensure peace, stability, and security in my future.

Aries

17 September 2025

Dear Aries, creativity is heightened today, making it a great time to explore new ideas and express your vision. Whether you're working on personal projects, solving challenges, or pursuing artistic endeavors, today's energy supports bold, imaginative thinking. Let your creativity guide you toward success.

Affirmation & Gratitude

I trust in my creativity, knowing that bold ideas will lead to exciting breakthroughs and fulfilling outcomes.

Aries

18 September 2025

Dear Aries, relationships take priority today, and the cosmos supports building deeper emotional connections with loved ones. Whether you're reconnecting with family, spending time with friends, or focusing on a romantic relationship, meaningful conversations will strengthen your bonds. Be open and empathetic in your interactions.

Affirmation & Gratitude

I nurture my relationships with love, honesty, and empathy, creating deeper emotional bonds with those who bring joy into my life.

Aries

19 September 2025

Dear Aries, career progress is highlighted today, and the energy supports making bold moves toward your professional goals. Whether you're seeking new responsibilities, expanding your skills, or exploring new opportunities, today's energy favors proactive action. Stay confident and trust your abilities.

Affirmation & Gratitude

I trust in my hard work and dedication, knowing they will lead to career success and personal fulfillment.

Aries

20 September 2025

Dear Aries, financial planning is in focus today, and the cosmos encourages you to make responsible decisions that align with your long-term financial goals. Whether you're reassessing your budget or preparing for a significant purchase, thoughtful financial planning today will bring peace and stability.

Affirmation & Gratitude

I make responsible financial decisions that ensure peace, stability, and security in my future.

Aries

21 September 2025

Dear Aries, creativity is heightened today, making it a great time to explore new ideas and bring your vision to life. Whether you're working on personal projects, solving challenges, or pursuing artistic endeavors, today's energy supports bold, imaginative thinking. Trust your instincts and let your creativity guide you toward success.

Affirmation & Gratitude

I trust in my creativity, knowing that bold ideas will lead to exciting breakthroughs and fulfilling outcomes.

Aries

22 September 2025

Dear Aries, relationships take focus today, and the cosmos encourages you to nurture emotional connections with loved ones. Whether you're reconnecting with family, spending time with friends, or focusing on a romantic relationship, meaningful conversations will strengthen your relationships. Be open, honest, and empathetic in your interactions.

Affirmation & Gratitude

I nurture my relationships with love, honesty, and gratitude, creating deeper emotional bonds with those who bring joy into my life.

Aries

23 September 2025

Dear Aries, career growth is in the spotlight today, and the energy supports making bold moves toward your professional goals. Whether you're seeking a promotion, expanding your responsibilities, or exploring new opportunities, today's energy favors proactive action. Stay confident in your abilities.

Affirmation & Gratitude

I trust in my skills and dedication, knowing they will lead to career success and personal fulfillment.

Aries

24 September 2025

Dear Aries, financial matters take focus today, and the cosmos supports making responsible decisions that align with your long-term financial goals. Whether you're reassessing your budget or saving for future investments, thoughtful financial choices today will bring peace and stability.

Affirmation & Gratitude

I make responsible financial decisions that ensure peace, stability, and security in my future.

Aries

25 September 2025

Dear Aries, creativity flows effortlessly today, making it the perfect time to explore new ideas and express your vision. Whether you're working on personal projects, solving challenges, or pursuing artistic endeavors, today's energy supports bold, imaginative thinking. Let your creativity lead the way.

Affirmation & Gratitude

I trust in my creativity, knowing that bold ideas will lead to exciting breakthroughs and fulfilling outcomes.

Aries

26 September 2025

Dear Aries, relationships take focus today, and the cosmos encourages you to nurture emotional connections with loved ones. Whether you're reconnecting with family or focusing on a romantic relationship, meaningful conversations will deepen your bonds. Be open, honest, and empathetic.

Affirmation & Gratitude

I nurture my relationships with love, honesty, and gratitude, creating deeper emotional bonds with those who bring joy into my life.

Aries

27 September 2025

Dear Aries, career advancement is highlighted today, and the energy supports making bold moves toward your professional goals. Whether you're seeking new responsibilities, expanding your skills, or exploring new opportunities, today's energy favors success. Stay confident and proactive in your approach.

Affirmation & Gratitude

I trust in my skills and dedication, knowing they will lead to career success and long-term fulfillment.

Aries

28 September 2025

Dear Aries, financial matters come into focus today, and the cosmos encourages you to make responsible decisions that align with your long-term financial goals. Whether you're reassessing your budget, saving for future investments, or preparing for a significant purchase, thoughtful financial planning today will bring peace and security.

Affirmation & Gratitude

I make responsible financial decisions that ensure peace, stability, and security in my future.

Aries

29 September 2025

Dear Aries, creativity is heightened today, making it an ideal time to explore new ideas and bring your vision to life. Whether you're working on personal projects, artistic endeavors, or solving challenges, today's energy supports bold, imaginative thinking. Trust your instincts and let your creativity lead you.

Affirmation & Gratitude

I trust in my creativity, knowing that bold ideas will lead to exciting breakthroughs and fulfilling outcomes.

Aries

30 September 2025

Dear Aries, relationships take priority today, and the cosmos encourages you to nurture emotional connections with loved ones. Whether you're reconnecting with family or focusing on friendships, meaningful conversations will strengthen your relationships. Be present and empathetic in your interactions.

Affirmation & Gratitude

I nurture my relationships with love, honesty, and gratitude, creating deeper emotional connections with those who bring joy into my life.

October

2025

Aries

1 October 2025

Dear Aries, creativity is in full swing today, making it the perfect time to explore new ideas and bring your vision to life. Whether you're working on personal projects or artistic endeavors, today's energy supports bold, imaginative thinking. Let your creativity guide you toward exciting breakthroughs.

Affirmation & Gratitude

I trust in my creativity, knowing that bold ideas will lead to exciting opportunities and fulfilling outcomes.

Aries

2 October 2025

Dear Aries, relationships take focus today, and the cosmos encourages you to nurture emotional connections with loved ones. Whether you're reconnecting with family or friends, meaningful conversations will strengthen your relationships. Be open, empathetic, and honest in your interactions.

Affirmation & Gratitude

I nurture my relationships with love, honesty, and empathy, creating deeper emotional connections with those who bring joy into my life.

Aries

3 October 2025

Dear Aries, career growth is highlighted today, and the energy supports making bold moves toward your professional aspirations. Whether you're seeking a promotion, expanding your responsibilities, or exploring new opportunities, today's energy favors proactive action. Stay confident in your abilities and take decisive steps toward success.

Affirmation & Gratitude

I trust in my skills and dedication, knowing they will lead to career success and personal fulfillment.

Aries

4 October 2025

Dear Aries, financial planning takes priority today, and the cosmos supports making responsible decisions that align with your long-term financial goals. Whether you're reassessing your budget or preparing for future investments, thoughtful financial planning today will bring peace and stability.

Affirmation & Gratitude

I make responsible financial decisions that ensure peace, stability, and security in my future.

Aries

5 October 2025

Dear Aries, creativity flows effortlessly today, making it a perfect time to explore new ideas and express your vision. Whether you're working on personal projects or artistic endeavors, today's energy supports bold, imaginative thinking. Let your creativity guide you toward success.

Affirmation & Gratitude

I trust in my creativity, knowing that bold ideas will lead to exciting breakthroughs and fulfilling outcomes.

Aries

6 October 2025

Dear Aries, relationships take priority today, and the cosmos encourages you to deepen emotional connections with loved ones. Whether you're spending time with family, friends, or focusing on a romantic bond, meaningful conversations will strengthen your relationships. Be present, empathetic, and open.

Affirmation & Gratitude

I nurture my relationships with love, honesty, and gratitude, creating deeper emotional bonds with those who bring joy into my life.

Aries

7 October 2025

Dear Aries, career progress is highlighted today, and the energy supports making bold moves toward your professional goals. Whether you're expanding your responsibilities, seeking a promotion, or exploring new opportunities, today's energy favors proactive action. Stay confident in your abilities and trust your dedication.

Affirmation & Gratitude

I trust in my skills and dedication, knowing they will lead to career success and long-term fulfillment.

Aries

8 October 2025

Dear Aries, financial matters take center stage today, and the cosmos encourages you to make responsible decisions that align with your long-term financial goals. Whether you're reassessing your budget or saving for future investments, today's energy supports thoughtful financial choices.

Affirmation & Gratitude

I make responsible financial decisions that ensure peace, stability, and security in my future.

Aries

9 October 2025

Dear Aries, creativity is heightened today, making it a great time to explore new ideas and bring your vision to life. Whether you're working on personal projects, solving challenges, or pursuing artistic endeavors, today's energy supports bold, imaginative thinking. Let your creativity guide you toward exciting breakthroughs.

Affirmation & Gratitude

I trust in my creativity, knowing that bold ideas will lead to exciting breakthroughs and fulfilling outcomes.

Aries

10 October 2025

Dear Aries, relationships take focus today, and the cosmos encourages you to nurture emotional connections with loved ones. Whether you're reconnecting with family or focusing on friendships, meaningful conversations will strengthen your relationships. Be open, honest, and empathetic.

Affirmation & Gratitude

I nurture my relationships with love, honesty, and gratitude, creating deeper emotional bonds with those who bring joy into my life.

Aries

11 October 2025

Dear Aries, career growth is highlighted today, and the energy supports making bold moves toward your professional aspirations. Whether you're seeking a promotion, expanding your skills, or exploring new opportunities, today's energy favors proactive action. Stay confident in your abilities.

Affirmation & Gratitude

I trust in my skills and dedication, knowing they will lead to career success and personal fulfillment.

Aries

12 October 2025

Dear Aries, financial planning takes priority today, and the cosmos supports making responsible decisions that align with your long-term financial goals. Whether you're reassessing your budget or preparing for a significant purchase, thoughtful financial choices today will bring peace and stability.

Affirmation & Gratitude

I make thoughtful financial decisions that ensure peace, stability, and security in my future.

Aries

13 October 2025

Dear Aries, creativity flows effortlessly today, making it a perfect time to explore new ideas and bring your vision to life. Whether you're working on personal projects, solving challenges, or pursuing artistic endeavors, today's energy supports bold, imaginative thinking. Let your creativity guide you.

Affirmation & Gratitude

I trust in my creativity, knowing that bold ideas will lead to exciting breakthroughs and fulfilling outcomes.

Aries

14 October 2025

Dear Aries, relationships take focus today, and the cosmos encourages you to nurture emotional connections with loved ones. Whether you're spending time with family or focusing on a romantic bond, meaningful conversations will strengthen your relationships. Be open, honest, and empathetic.

Affirmation & Gratitude

I nurture my relationships with love, honesty, and empathy, creating deeper emotional connections with those who bring joy into my life.

Aries

15 October 2025

Dear Aries, career advancement is within reach today, and the energy supports making bold moves toward your professional goals. Whether you're expanding your responsibilities, seeking a promotion, or exploring new opportunities, today's energy favors proactive action. Stay confident and proactive in your approach.

Affirmation & Gratitude

I trust in my skills and dedication, knowing they will lead to career success and long-term fulfillment.

Aries

16 October 2025

Dear Aries, financial matters take center stage today, and the energy supports making responsible decisions that align with your long-term financial goals. Whether you're reassessing your budget, saving for future investments, or preparing for a significant purchase, thoughtful financial planning will bring peace and stability.

Affirmation & Gratitude

I make responsible financial decisions that ensure peace, stability, and security in my future.

Aries

17 October 2025

Dear Aries, creativity is heightened today, making it a great time to explore new ideas and express your vision. Whether you're working on personal projects, solving challenges, or pursuing artistic endeavors, today's energy supports bold, imaginative thinking. Let your creativity guide you toward exciting breakthroughs.

Affirmation & Gratitude

I trust in my creativity, knowing that bold ideas will lead to exciting breakthroughs and fulfilling outcomes.

Aries

18 October 2025

Dear Aries, relationships take priority today, and the energy supports building deeper emotional connections with loved ones. Whether you're reconnecting with family, nurturing friendships, or focusing on a romantic bond, meaningful conversations will strengthen your relationships. Be present and empathetic.

Affirmation & Gratitude

I nurture my relationships with love, honesty, and gratitude, creating deeper emotional bonds with those who bring joy into my life.

Aries

19 October 2025

Dear Aries, career progress is highlighted today, and the energy supports making bold moves toward your professional goals. Whether you're expanding your responsibilities or exploring new opportunities, today's energy favors proactive action. Stay confident in your abilities and trust your dedication.

Affirmation & Gratitude

I trust in my hard work and dedication, knowing they will lead to career success and personal fulfillment.

Aries

20 October 2025

Dear Aries, financial matters come into focus today, and the cosmos encourages you to make responsible decisions that align with your long-term financial goals. Whether you're reassessing your budget or saving for future investments, thoughtful financial planning will bring peace and stability.

Affirmation & Gratitude

I make responsible financial decisions that ensure peace, stability, and security in my future.

Aries

21 October 2025

Dear Aries, creativity is heightened today, making it a great time to explore new ideas and express your vision. Whether you're working on personal projects, artistic endeavors, or solving challenges, today's energy supports bold, imaginative thinking. Let your creativity flow freely.

Affirmation & Gratitude

I trust in my creativity, knowing that bold ideas will lead to exciting breakthroughs and fulfilling outcomes.

Aries

22 October 2025

Dear Aries, relationships take focus today, and the cosmos encourages you to nurture emotional connections with loved ones. Whether you're reconnecting with family, spending time with friends, or focusing on a romantic bond, meaningful conversations will strengthen your relationships. Be open, honest, and empathetic in your interactions.

Affirmation & Gratitude

I nurture my relationships with love, honesty, and gratitude, creating deeper emotional connections with those who bring joy into my life.

Aries

23 October 2025

Dear Aries, career growth is highlighted today, and the energy supports making bold moves toward your professional goals. Whether you're seeking a promotion, expanding your responsibilities, or exploring new opportunities, today's energy favors proactive action. Stay confident in your abilities.

Affirmation & Gratitude

I trust in my skills and dedication, knowing they will lead to career success and personal fulfillment.

Aries

24 October 2025

Dear Aries, financial matters take focus today, and the cosmos encourages you to make responsible decisions that align with your long-term financial goals. Whether you're reassessing your budget or preparing for future investments, thoughtful financial planning today will bring peace and stability.

Affirmation & Gratitude

I make responsible financial decisions that ensure peace, stability, and security in my future.

Aries

25 October 2025

Dear Aries, creativity flows effortlessly today, making it a great time to explore new ideas and express your vision. Whether you're working on personal projects, solving challenges, or pursuing artistic endeavors, today's energy supports bold, imaginative thinking. Let your creativity guide you toward success.

Affirmation & Gratitude

I trust in my creativity, knowing that bold ideas will lead to exciting breakthroughs and fulfilling outcomes.

Aries

26 October 2025

Dear Aries, relationships take focus today, and the cosmos encourages you to nurture emotional connections with loved ones. Whether you're reconnecting with family or focusing on friendships, meaningful conversations will strengthen your relationships. Be present and empathetic in your interactions.

Affirmation & Gratitude

I nurture my relationships with love, honesty, and gratitude, creating deeper emotional connections with those who bring joy into my life.

Aries

27 October 2025

Dear Aries, career advancement is highlighted today, and the energy supports making bold moves toward your professional goals. Whether you're expanding your responsibilities, exploring new opportunities, or seeking new skills, today's energy favors proactive action. Stay focused and confident in your abilities.

Affirmation & Gratitude

I trust in my skills and dedication, knowing they will lead to career success and long-term fulfillment.

Aries

28 October 2025

Dear Aries, financial matters come into focus today, and the cosmos encourages you to make responsible decisions that align with your long-term financial goals. Whether you're saving for future investments, reassessing your budget, or preparing for a significant purchase, thoughtful financial choices today will bring peace and stability.

Affirmation & Gratitude

I make responsible financial decisions that ensure peace, stability, and security in my future.

Aries

29 October 2025

Dear Aries, creativity is heightened today, making it a perfect time to explore new ideas and bring your vision to life. Whether you're working on personal projects or artistic endeavors, today's energy supports bold, imaginative thinking. Let your creativity flow freely.

Affirmation & Gratitude

I trust in my creativity, knowing that bold ideas will lead to exciting breakthroughs and fulfilling outcomes.

Aries

30 October 2025

Dear Aries, relationships take focus today, and the cosmos encourages you to nurture emotional connections with loved ones. Whether you're reconnecting with family or focusing on friends, meaningful conversations will strengthen your bonds. Be open, honest, and empathetic in your interactions.

Affirmation & Gratitude

I nurture my relationships with love, honesty, and gratitude, creating deeper emotional connections with those who bring joy into my life.

Aries

31 October 2025

Dear Aries, career growth is in the spotlight today, and the energy supports making bold moves toward your professional aspirations. Whether you're seeking new responsibilities, expanding your skills, or exploring new opportunities, today's energy favors proactive action. Stay confident in your abilities.

Affirmation & Gratitude

I trust in my skills and dedication, knowing they will lead to career success and fulfillment.

November

2025

Aries

1 November 2025

Dear Aries, creativity is in full swing today, making it the perfect time to explore new ideas and bring your vision to life. Whether you're working on personal projects or artistic endeavors, today's energy supports bold, imaginative thinking. Let your creativity guide you toward exciting breakthroughs.

Affirmation & Gratitude

I trust in my creativity, knowing that bold ideas will lead to exciting opportunities and fulfilling outcomes.

Aries

2 November 2025

Dear Aries, relationships take focus today, and the cosmos encourages you to deepen emotional connections with loved ones. Whether you're spending time with family or nurturing friendships, meaningful conversations will strengthen your bonds. Be open, honest, and empathetic in your interactions.

Affirmation & Gratitude

I nurture my relationships with love, honesty, and empathy, creating deeper emotional bonds with those who bring joy into my life.

Aries

3 November 2025

Dear Aries, career growth is in the spotlight today, and the energy supports making bold moves toward your professional aspirations. Whether you're seeking a promotion, expanding your responsibilities, or exploring new opportunities, today's energy favors proactive action. Stay confident in your abilities.

Affirmation & Gratitude

I trust in my skills and hard work, knowing they will lead to career success and personal fulfillment.

Aries

4 November 2025

Dear Aries, financial planning takes priority today, and the cosmos supports making responsible decisions that align with your long-term financial goals. Whether you're reassessing your budget or preparing for future investments, thoughtful financial choices today will bring peace and stability.

Affirmation & Gratitude

I make responsible financial decisions that ensure peace, stability, and security in my future.

Aries

5 November 2025

Dear Aries, creativity flows effortlessly today, making it a great time to explore new ideas and express your vision. Whether you're working on personal projects, solving challenges, or pursuing artistic endeavors, today's energy supports bold, imaginative thinking. Let your creativity guide you toward exciting outcomes.

Affirmation & Gratitude

I trust in my creativity, knowing that bold ideas will lead to exciting breakthroughs and fulfilling outcomes.

Aries

6 November 2025

Dear Aries, relationships take focus today, and the cosmos encourages you to nurture emotional connections with loved ones. Whether you're reconnecting with family or focusing on friendships, meaningful conversations will strengthen your relationships. Be open, honest, and empathetic in your interactions.

Affirmation & Gratitude

I nurture my relationships with love, honesty, and gratitude, creating deeper emotional bonds with those who bring joy into my life.

Aries

7 November 2025

Dear Aries, career progress is highlighted today, and the energy supports making bold moves toward your professional goals. Whether you're expanding your responsibilities, seeking a promotion, or exploring new opportunities, today's energy favors proactive action. Stay confident in your abilities and trust your dedication.

Affirmation & Gratitude

I trust in my skills and dedication, knowing they will lead to career success and long-term fulfillment.

Aries

8 November 2025

Dear Aries, financial matters take center stage today, and the cosmos encourages you to make responsible decisions that align with your long-term financial goals. Whether you're reassessing your budget or saving for future investments, thoughtful financial planning today will bring peace and stability.

Affirmation & Gratitude

I make responsible financial decisions that ensure peace, stability, and security in my future.

Aries

9 November 2025

Dear Aries, creativity is heightened today, making it the perfect time to explore new ideas and express your vision. Whether you're working on personal projects or solving challenges, today's energy supports bold, imaginative thinking. Trust your instincts and let your creativity guide you toward exciting breakthroughs.

Affirmation & Gratitude

I trust in my creativity, knowing that bold ideas will lead to exciting breakthroughs and fulfilling outcomes.

Aries

10 November 2025

Dear Aries, relationships take focus today, and the cosmos encourages you to nurture emotional connections with loved ones. Whether you're reconnecting with family or focusing on a romantic relationship, meaningful conversations will strengthen your bonds. Be present and empathetic in your interactions.

Affirmation & Gratitude

I nurture my relationships with love, honesty, and gratitude, creating deeper emotional connections with those who bring joy into my life.

Aries

11 November 2025

Dear Aries, career growth is highlighted today, and the energy supports making bold moves toward your professional aspirations. Whether you're seeking a promotion, expanding your responsibilities, or exploring new opportunities, today's energy favors proactive action. Stay confident in your abilities and take steps toward success.

Affirmation & Gratitude

I trust in my skills and dedication, knowing they will lead to career success and personal fulfillment.

Aries

12 November 2025

Dear Aries, financial planning takes priority today, and the cosmos supports making responsible decisions that align with your long-term financial goals. Whether you're reassessing your budget or preparing for future investments, today's energy favors thoughtful financial choices that will bring peace and stability.

Affirmation & Gratitude

I make responsible financial decisions that ensure peace, stability, and security in my future.

Aries

13 November 2025

Dear Aries, creativity flows effortlessly today, making it the perfect time to explore new ideas and bring your vision to life. Whether you're working on personal projects, solving challenges, or pursuing artistic endeavors, today's energy supports bold, imaginative thinking. Let your creativity guide you.

Affirmation & Gratitude

I trust in my creativity, knowing that bold ideas will lead to exciting breakthroughs and fulfilling outcomes.

Aries

14 November 2025

Dear Aries, relationships take focus today, and the cosmos encourages you to nurture emotional connections with loved ones. Whether you're spending time with family, friends, or focusing on a romantic relationship, meaningful conversations will strengthen your relationships. Be open, honest, and empathetic in your interactions.

Affirmation & Gratitude

I nurture my relationships with love, honesty, and empathy, creating deeper emotional connections with those who bring joy into my life.

Aries

15 November 2025

Dear Aries, career advancement is highlighted today, and the energy supports making bold moves toward your professional goals. Whether you're seeking a promotion, expanding your responsibilities, or exploring new opportunities, today's energy favors proactive action. Stay confident and proactive in your approach.

Affirmation & Gratitude

I trust in my skills and dedication, knowing they will lead to career success and long-term fulfillment.

Aries

16 November 2025

Dear Aries, financial matters take center stage today, and the energy supports making responsible decisions that align with your long-term financial goals. Whether you're reassessing your budget, saving for future investments, or preparing for a significant purchase, thoughtful financial planning today will bring peace and stability.

Affirmation & Gratitude

I make responsible financial decisions that ensure peace, stability, and security in my future.

Aries

17 November 2025

Dear Aries, creativity is heightened today, making it a great time to explore new ideas and express your vision. Whether you're working on personal projects, solving challenges, or pursuing artistic endeavors, today's energy supports bold, imaginative thinking. Let your creativity flow and guide you toward exciting breakthroughs.

Affirmation & Gratitude

I trust in my creativity, knowing that bold ideas will lead to exciting breakthroughs and fulfilling outcomes.

Aries

18 November 2025

Dear Aries, relationships take priority today, and the energy supports building deeper emotional connections with loved ones. Whether you're reconnecting with family or focusing on friendships, meaningful conversations will strengthen your bonds. Be present and empathetic in your interactions.

Affirmation & Gratitude

I nurture my relationships with love, honesty, and gratitude, creating deeper emotional bonds with those who bring joy into my life.

Aries

19 November 2025

Dear Aries, career progress is highlighted today, and the energy supports making bold moves toward your professional goals. Whether you're expanding your responsibilities, seeking a promotion, or exploring new opportunities, today's energy favors proactive action. Stay confident in your abilities and trust your dedication.

Affirmation & Gratitude

I trust in my hard work and dedication, knowing they will lead to career success and personal fulfillment.

Aries

20 November 2025

Dear Aries, financial matters come into focus today, and the cosmos encourages you to make responsible decisions that align with your long-term financial goals. Whether you're reassessing your budget, saving for future investments, or preparing for a significant purchase, thoughtful financial planning today will bring peace and stability.

Affirmation & Gratitude

I make responsible financial decisions that ensure peace, stability, and security in my future.

Aries

21 November 2025

Dear Aries, creativity is heightened today, making it the perfect time to explore new ideas and express your vision. Whether you're working on personal projects, artistic endeavors, or solving challenges, today's energy supports bold, imaginative thinking. Let your creativity guide you toward exciting breakthroughs.

Affirmation & Gratitude

I trust in my creativity, knowing that bold ideas will lead to exciting breakthroughs and fulfilling outcomes.

Aries

22 November 2025

Dear Aries, relationships take focus today, and the cosmos encourages you to nurture emotional connections with loved ones. Whether you're reconnecting with family or focusing on friendships, meaningful conversations will deepen your relationships. Be open, honest, and empathetic in your interactions.

Affirmation & Gratitude

I nurture my relationships with love, honesty, and gratitude, creating deeper emotional connections with those who bring joy into my life.

Aries

23 November 2025

Dear Aries, career growth is highlighted today, and the energy supports making bold moves toward your professional goals. Whether you're seeking a promotion, expanding your responsibilities, or exploring new opportunities, today's energy favors proactive action. Stay confident in your abilities and focus on your aspirations.

Affirmation & Gratitude

I trust in my skills and dedication, knowing they will lead to career success and personal fulfillment.

Aries

24 November 2025

Dear Aries, financial planning is in focus today, and the cosmos encourages you to make responsible decisions that align with your long-term financial goals. Whether you're reassessing your budget or preparing for future investments, thoughtful financial planning today will bring peace and stability.

Affirmation & Gratitude

I make responsible financial decisions that ensure peace, stability, and security in my future.

Aries

25 November 2025

Dear Aries, creativity flows effortlessly today, making it a great time to explore new ideas and express your vision. Whether you're working on personal projects, artistic endeavors, or solving challenges, today's energy supports bold, imaginative thinking. Let your creativity guide you toward success.

Affirmation & Gratitude

I trust in my creativity, knowing that bold ideas will lead to exciting breakthroughs and fulfilling outcomes.

Aries

26 November 2025

Dear Aries, relationships take priority today, and the cosmos encourages you to nurture emotional connections with loved ones. Whether you're reconnecting with family or focusing on a romantic bond, meaningful conversations will strengthen your relationships. Be open and empathetic in your interactions.

Affirmation & Gratitude

I nurture my relationships with love, honesty, and empathy, creating deeper emotional bonds with those who bring joy into my life.

Aries

27 November 2025

Dear Aries, career progress is highlighted today, and the cosmos encourages you to take bold steps toward your professional goals. Whether you're expanding your responsibilities, exploring new opportunities, or seeking a promotion, today's energy favors proactive action. Stay focused and confident in your abilities.

Affirmation & Gratitude

I trust in my skills and dedication, knowing they will lead to career success and long-term fulfillment.

Aries

28 November 2025

Dear Aries, financial matters take focus today, and the cosmos encourages you to make responsible decisions that align with your long-term financial goals. Whether you're reassessing your budget, saving for future investments, or preparing for a significant purchase, thoughtful financial planning will bring peace and security.

Affirmation & Gratitude

I make responsible financial decisions that ensure peace, stability, and security in my future.

Aries

29 November 2025

Dear Aries, creativity is heightened today, making it a great time to explore new ideas and bring your vision to life. Whether you're working on personal projects or solving challenges, today's energy supports bold, imaginative thinking. Let your creativity flow freely.

Affirmation & Gratitude

I trust in my creativity, knowing that bold ideas will lead to exciting breakthroughs and fulfilling outcomes.

Aries

30 November 2025

Dear Aries, relationships take focus today, and the cosmos encourages you to nurture emotional connections with loved ones. Whether you're reconnecting with family or focusing on friendships, meaningful conversations will strengthen your relationships. Be open, honest, and empathetic in your interactions.

Affirmation & Gratitude

I nurture my relationships with love, honesty, and gratitude, creating deeper emotional connections with those who bring joy into my life.

December

2025

Aries

1 November 2025

Dear Aries, creativity is in full swing today, making it the perfect time to explore new ideas and bring your vision to life. Whether you're working on personal projects or artistic endeavors, today's energy supports bold, imaginative thinking. Let your creativity guide you toward exciting breakthroughs.

Affirmation & Gratitude

I trust in my creativity, knowing that bold ideas will lead to exciting opportunities and fulfilling outcomes.

Aries

2 November 2025

Dear Aries, relationships take focus today, and the cosmos encourages you to deepen emotional connections with loved ones. Whether you're spending time with family or nurturing friendships, meaningful conversations will strengthen your bonds. Be open, honest, and empathetic in your interactions.

Affirmation & Gratitude

I nurture my relationships with love, honesty, and empathy, creating deeper emotional bonds with those who bring joy into my life.

Aries

3 November 2025

Dear Aries, career growth is in the spotlight today, and the energy supports making bold moves toward your professional aspirations. Whether you're seeking a promotion, expanding your responsibilities, or exploring new opportunities, today's energy favors proactive action. Stay confident in your abilities.

Affirmation & Gratitude

I trust in my skills and hard work, knowing they will lead to career success and personal fulfillment.

Aries

4 November 2025

Dear Aries, financial planning takes priority today, and the cosmos supports making responsible decisions that align with your long-term financial goals. Whether you're reassessing your budget or preparing for future investments, thoughtful financial choices today will bring peace and stability.

Affirmation & Gratitude

I make responsible financial decisions that ensure peace, stability, and security in my future.

Aries

5 November 2025

Dear Aries, creativity flows effortlessly today, making it a great time to explore new ideas and express your vision. Whether you're working on personal projects, solving challenges, or pursuing artistic endeavors, today's energy supports bold, imaginative thinking. Let your creativity guide you toward exciting outcomes.

Affirmation & Gratitude

I trust in my creativity, knowing that bold ideas will lead to exciting breakthroughs and fulfilling outcomes.

Aries

6 November 2025

Dear Aries, relationships take focus today, and the cosmos encourages you to nurture emotional connections with loved ones. Whether you're reconnecting with family or focusing on friendships, meaningful conversations will strengthen your relationships. Be open, honest, and empathetic in your interactions.

Affirmation & Gratitude

I nurture my relationships with love, honesty, and gratitude, creating deeper emotional bonds with those who bring joy into my life.

Aries

7 November 2025

Dear Aries, career progress is highlighted today, and the energy supports making bold moves toward your professional goals. Whether you're expanding your responsibilities, seeking a promotion, or exploring new opportunities, today's energy favors proactive action. Stay confident in your abilities and trust your dedication.

Affirmation & Gratitude

I trust in my skills and dedication, knowing they will lead to career success and long-term fulfillment.

Aries

8 November 2025

Dear Aries, financial matters take center stage today, and the cosmos encourages you to make responsible decisions that align with your long-term financial goals. Whether you're reassessing your budget or saving for future investments, thoughtful financial planning today will bring peace and stability.

Affirmation & Gratitude

I make responsible financial decisions that ensure peace, stability, and security in my future.

Aries

9 November 2025

Dear Aries, creativity is heightened today, making it the perfect time to explore new ideas and express your vision. Whether you're working on personal projects or solving challenges, today's energy supports bold, imaginative thinking. Trust your instincts and let your creativity guide you toward exciting breakthroughs.

Affirmation & Gratitude

I trust in my creativity, knowing that bold ideas will lead to exciting breakthroughs and fulfilling outcomes.

Aries

10 November 2025

Dear Aries, relationships take focus today, and the cosmos encourages you to nurture emotional connections with loved ones. Whether you're reconnecting with family or focusing on a romantic relationship, meaningful conversations will strengthen your bonds. Be present and empathetic in your interactions.

Affirmation & Gratitude

I nurture my relationships with love, honesty, and gratitude, creating deeper emotional connections with those who bring joy into my life.

Aries

11 November 2025

Dear Aries, career growth is highlighted today, and the energy supports making bold moves toward your professional aspirations. Whether you're seeking a promotion, expanding your responsibilities, or exploring new opportunities, today's energy favors proactive action. Stay confident in your abilities and take steps toward success.

Affirmation & Gratitude

I trust in my skills and dedication, knowing they will lead to career success and personal fulfillment.

Aries

12 November 2025

Dear Aries, financial planning takes priority today, and the cosmos supports making responsible decisions that align with your long-term financial goals. Whether you're reassessing your budget or preparing for future investments, today's energy favors thoughtful financial choices that will bring peace and stability.

Affirmation & Gratitude

I make responsible financial decisions that ensure peace, stability, and security in my future.

Aries

13 November 2025

Dear Aries, creativity flows effortlessly today, making it the perfect time to explore new ideas and bring your vision to life. Whether you're working on personal projects, solving challenges, or pursuing artistic endeavors, today's energy supports bold, imaginative thinking. Let your creativity guide you.

Affirmation & Gratitude

I trust in my creativity, knowing that bold ideas will lead to exciting breakthroughs and fulfilling outcomes.

Aries

14 November 2025

Dear Aries, relationships take focus today, and the cosmos encourages you to nurture emotional connections with loved ones. Whether you're spending time with family, friends, or focusing on a romantic relationship, meaningful conversations will strengthen your relationships. Be open, honest, and empathetic in your interactions.

Affirmation & Gratitude

I nurture my relationships with love, honesty, and empathy, creating deeper emotional connections with those who bring joy into my life.

Aries

15 November 2025

Dear Aries, career advancement is highlighted today, and the energy supports making bold moves toward your professional goals. Whether you're seeking a promotion, expanding your responsibilities, or exploring new opportunities, today's energy favors proactive action. Stay confident and proactive in your approach.

Affirmation & Gratitude

I trust in my skills and dedication, knowing they will lead to career success and long-term fulfillment.

Aries

16 November 2025

Dear Aries, financial matters take center stage today, and the energy supports making responsible decisions that align with your long-term financial goals. Whether you're reassessing your budget, saving for future investments, or preparing for a significant purchase, thoughtful financial planning today will bring peace and stability.

Affirmation & Gratitude

I make responsible financial decisions that ensure peace, stability, and security in my future.

Aries

17 November 2025

Dear Aries, creativity is heightened today, making it a great time to explore new ideas and express your vision. Whether you're working on personal projects, solving challenges, or pursuing artistic endeavors, today's energy supports bold, imaginative thinking. Let your creativity flow and guide you toward exciting breakthroughs.

Affirmation & Gratitude

I trust in my creativity, knowing that bold ideas will lead to exciting breakthroughs and fulfilling outcomes.

Aries

18 November 2025

Dear Aries, relationships take priority today, and the energy supports building deeper emotional connections with loved ones. Whether you're reconnecting with family or focusing on friendships, meaningful conversations will strengthen your bonds. Be present and empathetic in your interactions.

Affirmation & Gratitude

I nurture my relationships with love, honesty, and gratitude, creating deeper emotional bonds with those who bring joy into my life.

Aries

19 November 2025

Dear Aries, career progress is highlighted today, and the energy supports making bold moves toward your professional goals. Whether you're expanding your responsibilities, seeking a promotion, or exploring new opportunities, today's energy favors proactive action. Stay confident in your abilities and trust your dedication.

Affirmation & Gratitude

I trust in my hard work and dedication, knowing they will lead to career success and personal fulfillment.

Aries

20 November 2025

Dear Aries, financial matters come into focus today, and the cosmos encourages you to make responsible decisions that align with your long-term financial goals. Whether you're reassessing your budget, saving for future investments, or preparing for a significant purchase, thoughtful financial planning today will bring peace and stability.

Affirmation & Gratitude

I make responsible financial decisions that ensure peace, stability, and security in my future.

Aries

21 November 2025

Dear Aries, creativity is heightened today, making it the perfect time to explore new ideas and express your vision. Whether you're working on personal projects, artistic endeavors, or solving challenges, today's energy supports bold, imaginative thinking. Let your creativity guide you toward exciting breakthroughs.

Affirmation & Gratitude

I trust in my creativity, knowing that bold ideas will lead to exciting breakthroughs and fulfilling outcomes.

Aries

22 November 2025

Dear Aries, relationships take focus today, and the cosmos encourages you to nurture emotional connections with loved ones. Whether you're reconnecting with family or focusing on friendships, meaningful conversations will deepen your relationships. Be open, honest, and empathetic in your interactions.

Affirmation & Gratitude

I nurture my relationships with love, honesty, and gratitude, creating deeper emotional connections with those who bring joy into my life.

Aries

23 November 2025

Dear Aries, career growth is highlighted today, and the energy supports making bold moves toward your professional goals. Whether you're seeking a promotion, expanding your responsibilities, or exploring new opportunities, today's energy favors proactive action. Stay confident in your abilities and focus on your aspirations.

Affirmation & Gratitude

I trust in my skills and dedication, knowing they will lead to career success and personal fulfillment.

Aries

24 November 2025

Dear Aries, financial planning is in focus today, and the cosmos encourages you to make responsible decisions that align with your long-term financial goals. Whether you're reassessing your budget or preparing for future investments, thoughtful financial planning today will bring peace and stability.

Affirmation & Gratitude

I make responsible financial decisions that ensure peace, stability, and security in my future.

Aries

25 November 2025

Dear Aries, creativity flows effortlessly today, making it a great time to explore new ideas and express your vision. Whether you're working on personal projects, artistic endeavors, or solving challenges, today's energy supports bold, imaginative thinking. Let your creativity guide you toward success.

Affirmation & Gratitude

I trust in my creativity, knowing that bold ideas will lead to exciting breakthroughs and fulfilling outcomes.

Aries

26 November 2025

Dear Aries, relationships take priority today, and the cosmos encourages you to nurture emotional connections with loved ones. Whether you're reconnecting with family or focusing on a romantic bond, meaningful conversations will strengthen your relationships. Be open and empathetic in your interactions.

Affirmation & Gratitude

I nurture my relationships with love, honesty, and empathy, creating deeper emotional bonds with those who bring joy into my life.

Aries

27 November 2025

Dear Aries, career progress is highlighted today, and the cosmos encourages you to take bold steps toward your professional goals. Whether you're expanding your responsibilities, exploring new opportunities, or seeking a promotion, today's energy favors proactive action. Stay focused and confident in your abilities.

Affirmation & Gratitude

I trust in my skills and dedication, knowing they will lead to career success and long-term fulfillment.

Aries

28 November 2025

Dear Aries, financial matters take focus today, and the cosmos encourages you to make responsible decisions that align with your long-term financial goals. Whether you're reassessing your budget, saving for future investments, or preparing for a significant purchase, thoughtful financial planning will bring peace and security.

Affirmation & Gratitude

I make responsible financial decisions that ensure peace, stability, and security in my future.

Aries

29 November 2025

Dear Aries, creativity is heightened today, making it a great time to explore new ideas and bring your vision to life. Whether you're working on personal projects or solving challenges, today's energy supports bold, imaginative thinking. Let your creativity flow freely.

Affirmation & Gratitude

I trust in my creativity, knowing that bold ideas will lead to exciting breakthroughs and fulfilling outcomes.

Aries

30 November 2025

Dear Aries, relationships take focus today, and the cosmos encourages you to nurture emotional connections with loved ones. Whether you're reconnecting with family or focusing on friendships, meaningful conversations will strengthen your relationships. Be open, honest, and empathetic in your interactions.

Affirmation & Gratitude

I nurture my relationships with love, honesty, and gratitude, creating deeper emotional connections with those who bring joy into my life.

The Answers You Seek

Are Within

The "Daily Guidance" series offers an innovative approach to finding spiritual wisdom and practical advice. Each book in the series is a unique tool designed for daily introspection and decision-making. Readers are invited to meditate on a question or seek general guidance for the day, then flip to a random page in the book. The page they land on provides a personalized message from various spiritual sources, such as angels, tarot, or spirit animals. With each turn of the page, these books deliver insightful, positive messages and mantras to inspire personal growth and provide clarity on life's daily challenges and decisions.

Other books in this series:-
The Angelic Oracles
Daily Angel Tarot Reading
Mystic Tarot Cat
Oracle of the Tarot Cat
Vibes Unveiled
Spirit Animal Oracle
Answers from the Oracles
Messages from the Angels

Daily Guidance
SERIES

Unlock the stars and save!

Get 20% off

my 2025 Horoscope Guide Collection

Use code

STARS2025GUIDE

Perfect for personal guidance or as a gift only at: -

www.korupublishing.com